Joseph Lord

Israel's judicial blindness

and the public and unexplained parables of our Lord

Joseph Lord

Israel's judicial blindness
and the public and unexplained parables of our Lord

ISBN/EAN: 9783744740647

Printed in Europe, USA, Canada, Australia, Japan

Cover: Foto ©Lupo / pixelio.de

More available books at **www.hansebooks.com**

Israel's Judicial Blindness;

AND THE

PUBLIC AND UNEXPLAINED PARABLES OF OUR LORD.

THEIR PLACE IN INSPIRED PROPHECY.

BY JOSEPH L. LORD, M. A.,

OF THE BOSTON BAR,

Author of "Briefs on Prophetic Themes," etc.

~~~~~~~~~~~~~~~

Ἰδοὺ, ὁ νυμφίος ἔρχεται.—MATT. XXV, 6.

~~~~~~~~~~~~~~~

PHILADELPHIA:
CHARLES W. QUICK.
FOR SALE AT
THE PROTESTANT EPISCOPAL BOOK STORE, 124 CHESTNUT STREET,
ALSO BY
E. P. DUTTON & CO., 135 WASHINGTON STREET, BOSTON,
AND
762 BROADWAY, NEW YORK.
1868.

INTRODUCTORY NOTE.

The treatise on the subject indicated by the title-page, and contained in the following pages, was first published in the supplementary columns of THE EPISCOPALIAN. The Editor of that journal begs leave to make mention of the wide-spread interest which its perusal has caused, and to testify to the many and high commendations which have reached him from Bible students well qualified to judge of the merits of such a work. A just enumeration of those merits must include the literary qualities of the essay. The clearness of expression, the strength and purity of language and the nervousness of style will not fail to attract and please all persons of cultivated and refined taste.

The modest and unpretending volume is offered as a contribution to the study of the prophecies relating to "the ancient people," now daily rising into importance, and drawing to themselves such earnest thought and close attention.

The main feature of the treatise will not fail to strike the mind of the reader, and he will be pleased to find Scripture interpreting itself, and all the rays of distinct prophetic instructions, relating to the judicial blindness of Israel, united and condensed in the focal point assigned to our Lord's unexplained parables. The collocation of the words of Him who spake as never man spake, delivered by His Own mouth, with those words, also His Own, but uttered by the prophets under the inspiration of His Spirit, must be highly suggestive; while the clearness, precision and force of the logical sequence between the passages of Scripture cited, and the inferences of fact derived therefrom, must strongly impress the mind of the reader, even if he should not feel prepared, without further inquiry (which the author himself earnestly solicits), to give a ready assent to all the conclusions of the author, in the form and related order in which they are set forth in the summing-up at the close of his discussion.

His readers will find they have entered a different atmosphere when they turn from the strife of controversy to peruse these pages. The position of the thinker seems to us to be like that of the Lord's people in the days of Malachi; "They that feared the Lord spake often one to another: and the Lord hearkened and heard it."

It will be discovered by the reader that the author has not entered the mazes of chronology, nor attempted to assign definite dates to the fulfilment of prophecies. Such definite epochs doubtless exist in the divine counsels, and many of them are found stated with precision and others symbolically and metaphorically in various parts of the Scriptures. The great difficulty is to find the key to those clearly-defined epochs, and to settle conclusively the beginning or ending of any one.

It is suggested, at this point, that the hour when the sentence of judicial blindness was pronounced by Isaiah, or the time when it began to be executed, was the beginning of that epoch terminating with the close of the times of the Gentiles, and corresponding with the "seven times" mentioned by Moses (Levit. xxvi, 18-24). Can either period be ascertained?

The volume is now committed to the candid and prayerful attention of the reader, with the assured belief that the Divine blessing will attend its perusal.

C. W. Q.

PREFACE.

For twenty-six hundred years, the sentence of judicial blindness has hung, like a funeral pall, over the Jewish mind, covering the whole earth, wherever Israel has been scattered (and where has Israel not been scattered?) with its thick and ample folds.

Ever after this sentence was pronounced by the prophet Isaiah, all the prophecies, both judicial and millennial, of the Old Testament, and all the prophecies of our Saviour in the New Testament, so far as Israel is concerned, either presuppose, or are directly based upon, the great fact of her judicial blindness, until the close of her present judicial dispensation.

Of no class of prophecies can this be said with greater truth, than of those contained in the public and unexplained parables of our Lord.

The connection of these parables with the judicial blindness of Israel—which blindness is the reason given by our Saviour to His disciples, why He spake to the Jewish multitudes in parables—does not seem to us to have received that degree of attention from writers on the parables, which its prophetic importance properly demands.

Hence these pages, revised from the columns of THE EPISCOPALIAN: the object of which has been to supply in some measure, though very briefly and imperfectly, and without any attempt at elaborate discussion, any deficiency which may have been felt by other minds in

the same regard ; our object being rather to suggest
and elicit, and not by any means to satisfy or exhaust
inquiry.

As is becoming in a layman, we have affected not the
traditions of the fathers, or the learning, or the methods
of the schools ; but, without disrespect thereto, have
sought only for what have appeared to us to be the plain
teachings of the Word and providence of God on the
subject, which, as one in a series, we have chosen for
our present theme, in the full persuasion, if these teachings are what we have represented them to be, that they
were never of greater practical consequence to all concerned, to Jews and Gentiles both, than at the present
day.

May the God of Israel hearken and hear, and own
and bless the words which we have written.

JOSEPH L. LORD.

Saxonville, Mass., June, 1868.

Israel's Judicial Blindness.

ISRAEL'S JUDICIAL BLINDNESS.

"Therefore speak I unto them in parables; because seeing they see not, and hearing they hear not, neither do they understand. And in them is fulfilled the prophecy of Esaias, which saith, By hearing ye shall hear, and shall not understand; and seeing, ye shall see and shall not perceive: for this people's heart is waxed gross, and their ears are dull of hearing, and their eyes they have closed; lest at any time they should see with their eyes, and hear with their ears, and should understand with their heart, and should be converted, and I should heal them" (Matt. xiii, 13-15).

The parables of the New Testament are confined to the personal teachings of our Saviour.

According to the enumeration of Trench they are thirty in number; according to Greswell twenty-seven only.

In the present discussion we shall adopt the enumeration of Mr. Greswell, though their precise number is not of consequence to our purpose.

We do not propose to discuss the nature of parables in general, or as a distinct form of our Saviour's instructions; nor do we propose to discuss any general or particular classification or feature of them, or any distinction existing between them, except that only which is denoted by our title and by the plain letter of the record; namely, that some of them were explained by our Saviour when He uttered them, and that others were left wholly unexplained by Him, whatever may have been recorded in connection therewith by the inspired historians who relate them. This, it will be observed, is not a speculative distinction, but a difference of fact only.

It is well to observe, however, that the explained parables form integral parts of continuous discourses of our Saviour, not in the least interrupting, but rather rendering more complete, the flowing narrative; while, on the other hand, the unexplained parables are introduced abruptly, and break in upon the connected order of the sacred narrative, without any assigned cause for the obvious interruption, or any clue afforded by any accompanying note or comment of our Saviour, by which His hearers might, as in the case of the explained parables, readily interpret their hidden meaning and design.

It will, we think, appear, as we proceed with our discussion, that the unexplained parables are strictly prophetic and historical in their office and character; relating not, like the explained parables, to timely precepts, or present duties and obligations, but to future events only; not to what, in point of moral duty, a particular course of conduct should be, but to what, in point of fact, the inevitable results of a given course of moral conduct will be; and that, not so much in reference to individuals, as to mankind, or some one or more of the great Scriptural divisions of mankind at large.

It will, we think, not only appear that the unexplained parables are thus strictly prophetic in their office and character, but that, equally with other distinct classes of prophecy, they have their own peculiar place and sphere among the prophetic oracles of the Holy Scriptures, and form a distinct class by themselves; looking, however, not less than other prophecy, to a certain moral state of things, and to a certain moral condition of life and character in those to whom they are addressed, and at the time they are addressed, for the full vindication of the wisdom of their use; but to the course of future events only, for the full and final unfolding and clearing up of their hidden meaning and design.

Of the unexplained parables, however, we propose to discuss those only which were intended for the Jewish nation at large, and were therefore addressed either to public and mixed assemblies of the Jews, or to the Scribes and Pharisees as the more notable representatives of the nation, and the constant and inveterate enemies and persecutors of our Saviour.

It is not as yet of account to our general theme, that some of the public and unexplained parables were, after their delivery, privately explained by our Saviour, in respect to their general scope and signification, to His disciples. That they were thus privately explained, though of great account undoubtedly to the disciples at the time, as it will be to us when we come to their exposition, was of no account to those to whom they were especially addressed, and helped not to enlighten their blinded moral understanding, either as to their prophetic character, or as to the reason (privately explained to the disciples) why our Saviour made use of this particular form of prophecy so largely to the exclusion of all other forms, when, in the middle of the second year of His ministry, He first began to speak to the nation in parables.

The seven explained, or doctrinal and ethical parables, with the moral taught by each, are as follows: 1. The king who took account of his debtors; or, the duty of forgiveness. 2. The good Samaritan; or, the true nature of love to our neighbor. 3. The rich fool; or, the folly of putting our trust in earthly riches. 4. The unjust steward; or, our accountability to God for the use of earthly riches. 5. The rich man and Lazarus; or, the fatal folly of perverting earthly riches to the good things of this life, its self-indulgent pleasures and luxuries, its costly and voluptuous living. 6. The importunate widow; or, the duty of perseverance and importunity in prayer. 7. The Pharisee and publican; or, the supreme folly of self-righteousness; of self-complacency and self-ostentation in respect to our religious character and attainments.

The precise prophetic and historic import of the unexplained parables, on the other hand, (we do not need, at present, to make any distinction between those which were addressed 'to the Jewish public and those which were addressed to the disciples in private) is not susceptible of being either so briefly denoted, or so readily determined, but must await their separate exposition. They are as follows:—

1. The sower and his seed (Matt. xiii, 1–9; Mark iv, 1–9; Luke viii, 4–8).

2. The tares of the field (Matt. xiii, 24–30).

3. The seed growing secretly (Mark iv, 26–29).

4. The grain of mustard-seed (Matt. xiii, 31, 32; Mark iv, 30–32; Luke xiii, 18, 19).

5. The leaven (Matt. xiii, 33; Luke xiii, 20, 21).

6. The hidden treasure (Matt. xiii, 44).

7. The pearl (Matt. xiii, 45, 46).

8. The draw-net cast into the sea (Matt. xiii, 47, 48).

9. The good shepherd (John x, 1–18).

10, 11. The servants left in wait for their lord; and the servant left instead of his lord (Luke xii, 22–48).

12. The barren fig-tree (Luke xiii, 1–9).

13. The great supper (Luke xiv, 15–24).

14. The prodigal son (Luke xv, 11–32).

15. The laborers in the vineyard (Matt. xx, 1–16).

16. The ten pieces of money, or the pounds (Luke xix, 11–27).

17. The wicked husbandmen (Matt. xxi, 33–44; Mark xii, 1–11; Luke xx, 9–18).

18. The marriage of the king's son, or the wedding garment (Matt. xxii, 1–14).

19, 20. The ten virgins; and the talents (Matt. xxv, 1–30).

The parables in general, without reference to any particular classification of them, have often been compared to apples of gold in pictures of silver, of which the other teachings of our Saviour form the silver setting. Be this as it may, it is now of consequence only to call the attention of our readers to the high and absolute importance of that portion of the parables, and that strictly in reference to their prophetic office and character, which is denoted by our title.

We do not notice any difference, and we are not aware that any exists, between the parables as we have thus distinguished them, in respect to their outward form and structure, or in respect to what would, at first sight, appear to be their obvious and *prima facie* signification. It now concerns us to notice only that some of them are briefly and pointedly explained by our Saviour, and that others are left by Him, on account of the judicial blindness of His hearers, wholly unexplained.

We notice, moreover, that those which are explained are uniformly employed by our Saviour for the purpose of preceptive or didactic instruction, as familiar practical examples, or cases in point, to illustrate and enforce particular maxims of Christian ethics, or particular rules of Christian duty, binding at the time and at all times, upon those to whom they were addressed, and upon all men.

We further notice that parables of this class do not in the least depend upon the course of future events for a ready, just and full apprehension of their true import and design, but upon the accompanying explanation of our Saviour alone; indeed, that the course of future events is expected to add nothing, and can add nothing, to the clearness, completeness and force of their meaning, as timely, pertinent and perpetual illustrations of ever-present duties and obligations; duties and obligations which, requiring no reference to the future, or to the past, belong to the case of every man, and to the ever-present now.

But we notice nothing of this kind in respect to the unexplained parables. Very true it is, that the unexplained parables are sometimes, like the explained

parables, loosely employed, in whole or in part, as
familiar illustrations of particular moral and Christian duties and obligations. It may be very well to
employ them in such subsidiary sense, or with such
ethical reference, but it should always be with a
manifest reservation ; for it is not well, in so em-
ploying them, to fail of their primary, their higher,
and their intended, though less obvious meaning and
design, which is more vast and far-reaching and con-
sequential by far. Indeed, remissness or misappre-
hension in this respect, is apt to lead us into grave
and dangerous errors in regard to the nature and
office, the divine and human relations, of Christ's
spiritual kingdom on the earth under the present
Gospel dispensation, and the dispensational results,
near and remote, which, according to prophecy, are
to be accomplished thereby : which results, as it
appears to us, it is the special province of the unexplained parables, both public and private, to foreshow.

In a certain sense all the teachings of our Saviour
are prophetic. His sermon on the mount is by some
expositors called the prophecy on the mount. So
also His various discourses to His disciples, especially His farewell discourses to them on the week of
His crucifixion; His discourse on the new birth to
Nicodemus; His denunciation of the Scribes and
Pharisees in the temple on the Wednesday evening
preceding His crucifixion ; and the explained parables themselves. Indeed, all the teachings of our
Saviour are prophetic in the sense of being applicable
at all times, during the whole rounded term of the
present Gospel dispensation, to the moral condition,
and spiritual wants and necessities of mankind, in
the various classes into which they are Scripturally
divided.

But the unexplained parables, both public and
private, are prophetic in a very different, and far
higher and closer sense; for they foreshow with the
most literal fidelity, at the very outset of the dispen-

sation, the actual and absolute results of the moral
conduct of mankind, in their relations to Christ's
spiritual kingdom, throughout the whole course of the
Gospel dispensation. They are a prospective history
of the moral conduct and acts of mankind, in their
relation to that kingdom, to the end of the dispensation ; precisely as, at the end of the dispensation, they
will be a retrospective history thereof, without the
necessity, at the end of the dispensation, of altering
a single word in which they were expressed at the
beginning of it; for known unto their Divine Author
were all things, past, present, and to come, from the
foundation of the world.

Does the reader desire Scriptural evidence of the
prophetic office and character of the unexplained
parables? Of course, the highest possible evidence,
which is tantamount to our Saviour's declaration to
this effect, is His private interpretation of some of
them to His disciples. He has thus, for example,
interpreted, in respect to their general scope and
meaning, without satisfying curiosity as to definite
particulars, the parables of the sower, the draw-net
and the tares.

Again; the running action, so to speak, of the three
last named and other unexplained parables embraces,
in express terms, the whole period of the Gospel dispensation, from its earliest seed-time to the final in-
gathering of its harvest. This is as true of the
unexplained parables which were not privately explained at the time of their delivery, or afterwards,
as of those which were privately explained ; as, for
example, those of the leaven, the servants left in
wait, the servant left instead of his lord, the pounds,
the ten virgins, the talents, etc.

Not less decisive evidence of their prophetic office
and character is afforded by the literal and exact
fulfilment, already accomplished, of the prophecies
which some of them contain. Thus the parable of
the wicked husbandmen was fulfilled to the letter by
the crucifixion of our Saviour, within three days after

it was uttered; while others, not wholly fulfilled as yet, are no less clearly in process of fulfilment.

Again; it is "the kingdom of God," or "kingdom of heaven;" that is, Christ's spiritual kingdom, or professing Church, under its present earthly form and manifestation; in its divine and human relations, or probationary relations, under the present Gospel dispensation, and throughout the whole course of it, without any limitation of time except the recorded limitation of the end of the dispensation; which is, in express terms, presented to us under the symbols and similitudes of a majority of the unexplained parables; which majority are uniformly introduced with the words, " The kingdom of God," or of " heaven," is like unto this or that symbol. These symbols and similitudes, being generalized by our Saviour into brief allegoric narratives of inimitable beauty, of strict fidelity to actual facts, and of wonderful concentration and comprehensiveness of meaning, therefore present to us a faithful outline, in advance, of the real, but (to the judicially-blinded minds of the Jewish nation, and to all judicially-blinded minds) concealed history of Christ's spiritual kingdom in its present earthly form and manifestation, throughout the whole course of the present Gospel dispensation, from the beginning to the end of it.

Finally; it was our Saviour's declared purpose (Matt. xiii, 10–16) to veil the hidden sense of His public and unexplained parables, and to conceal it entirely from the judicially-blinded minds of those to whom they were addressed; "lest at any time they should see with their eyes, and hear with their ears, and should understand with their heart, and should be converted, and I should heal them." This is remarkably true of one group of them, the first which He uttered, the group in regard to which He declared His purpose to conceal His meaning from His hearers. We refer to those recorded in the thirteenth chapter of Matthew.

Is it asked, why should our Saviour address these
parables to the Jewish multitudes, if they were intended for their instruction (as all the teachings of
our Saviour were), and were yet, when spoken, unin-
telligible to them, and intended so to be?

Was it not, we inquire in reply, because they
were intended, not for the *present*, but *future* instruction only, of the nation? because, in its present
judicial blindness, with which our Saviour never in-
terfered, but only reaffirmed, the nation was utterly
incapable of understanding the mysteries of Christ's
spiritual kingdom, which it was the special office
(Matt. xiii, 11) of the unexplained parables to un-
fold? and because, in the distant future, at the expiration of their sentence of judicial blindness, the
now hidden meaning of these parables would be sent
home to their now blinded minds by the stern and
irresistible logic of future events? Was it not that
when, at the close of the present dispensation, all the
prophecies of these parables, and all other judgments
against the guilty nation should be at last fulfilled,
and the sentence of their judicial blindness should
be ready to expire; that then, the promised "Spirit of
grace and of supplications" being poured upon them
(Zechariah xii, 10), they should be able, by means of
these prophetic landmarks, to more clearly discern
and trace all the way their long-suffering God
had both in judgment and in mercy led them, and
thus be convicted of their sins and brought to repentance?

In the time of our Saviour, the nation was sunk
in more profound judicial darkness than ever before. The little light that was in them was a greater
darkness than ever before. Not only had their sins
called down upon them, seven hundred and fifty years
before, the sentence of judicial blindness, as pronounced by the prophet Isaiah, but they had been
daily adding to it ever since, and were more than ever
adding to it now, in their blind hate and rage, by
their daily rejection of their Messiah and scornful

2

derision of Him as an impostor and pretender. Already was it in their hearts to crucify Him. The very day on which the first parable was uttered, they had very nearly, if not quite, committed the unpardonable sin of blaspheming the Holy Ghost, in this His own peculiar dispensation, by the impious accusation : "This fellow doth not cast out devils, but by Beelzebub the prince of the devils."

Moreover, it was now the middle of the second year of our Saviour's ministry, and all other means of reaching their impenetrable hearts had been resorted to in vain, and nothing was now left but to reiterate to the incorrigibly hardened and unbelieving nation their ancient and more than ever merited sentence of judicial blindness, and to reconsign them to the judicial and peremptory wrath of a holy and offended God. Nothing, in short, was now left, but to *foretell* to them, not what might be, but what beyond a peradventure, or possible alternative, should be, the certain and inevitable consequences of their infatuated blindness and unbelief; in the hope, the forlorn hope, forlorn but for God's ever faithful covenants with their fathers, that when, at the end of their judicial dispensation, they should have filled up the measure of their fathers, and all the prophetic judgments both of the Old Testament and the New should be fulfilled upon them, and they should then look upon Him whom they were now about to pierce; moved by "the Spirit of grace and of supplications," and overwhelmed by the unexpected reappearance of their crucified and still rejected Messiah, and by the infinite love that could not and would not give them up, even in the uttermost extremity of their sins and in the uttermost hour of a longer, and darker, and guiltier dispensation than that of their ancient and forfeited Theocracy; and appalled by the indictment, which the black record of their sins, running through the now completed term of two dispensations, would present against them ; they would then, at length, recognize and hail their crucified Messiah not less as

their pierced and bleeding Saviour, than as their
promised King, and mourn because of their rejection
of Him, in all the land, all their families apart, and
all their wives apart, as one mourneth for a first-born
and an only son; and hasten with one accord to the
fountain which in that day will be opened to the
house of David and to the inhabitants of Jerusalem
for sin and uncleanness, remembering all their evil
ways and their doings that were not good, and loath-
ing themselves in their own sight, for their iniquities
and their abominations.

It is not for us to speculate as to the reason why
our Saviour selected parables, a purely allegorical
form of prophecy, as being better adapted to the
judicial blindness of the nation, than a more direct
and literal method of communicating to them the
certain future consequences of their judicial blindness and their sins; but it is not difficult to conceive that the nation, in their blind hate and rage,
would not have tolerated His ministry another
hour, if the same truths had been told to them in a
plainer and more intelligible form. It is enough for
us, that our Saviour, in accordance with the invari-
able practice of Old-Testament prophecy, did
hold up to the nation the certain future consequences
of its judicial blindness and its sins, and that, for this
purpose, He employed a new and unaccustomed
form of prophecy, the allegorical form of parables,
as better adapted than any other to the changed
moral and spiritual relations of a new, and more
complex, and more spiritual dispensation, and to the
then moral condition of the nation.

But it is not necessary to dwell at greater length
upon the Scriptural evidence of the prophetic office
and character of the unexplained parables; for,
after all, their separate exposition, in the light of their
own and other Scripture testimony, is the most
satisfactory evidence which can be adduced, that
such is their office and character.

To correctly understand the prophetic application

of the unexplained parables, it is of great consequence to first place before our minds, as clearly and distinctly as possible, some of the leading Scriptural divisions of mankind, as contemplated by both the Old and New-Testament Scriptures, but especially, as concerning our present theme, by the unexplained parables. Of these divisions the four following are among the most prominent :—

1. The unbelieving, but covenanted, nation of the Jews.

2. The unbelieving, but uncovenanted, nations of the Gentiles.

3. The Professing Church.

4. The Elect Church or " remnant according to the election of grace," chosen out of the unbelieving Jewish and Gentile nations.

The two classes first named are often, though by no means always, spoken of in the Scriptures, in respect to their common unbelief, as forming one class only, but whenever they are spoken of in reference to the several Jewish covenants, they are carefully discriminated from one another.

The two classes last named, though often referred to in Scripture under the third head, are yet in other passages, and especially in the unexplained parables, carefully distinguished.

Our Saviour first offered to the unbelieving but covenanted Jewish nation in its judicial blindness, or, which is the same thing, to the professing, but wholly corrupt and apostate Jewish Church, which hitherto was His only visible Church on earth, *not* the Davidic and temporal kingdom which they had expected, and which had been promised to them, of which He was to be the Theocratic head, but of which in their sins they were as yet unworthy; but His spiritual kingdom only, and that only, on account of their sins, upon conditions which were as repugnant to their ceremonial self-righteousness, as it was to their infatuated worldly hopes and expectations.

The result was simply as had been foretold, and
as could only have been expected, that they rejected Him. blindly shutting against themselves the
graciously-opened door of His spiritual kingdom,
and its graciously-offered and free salvation. "Away
with Him, away with Him;" "Crucify Him, crucify
Him;" "His blood be on us and on our children;"
"we will not have this man to rule over us;" was
their cry. And despised and derided, rejected and
crucified, He returned to heaven, even as when His
Personal Divine Glory ascended thither, as seen by
the prophet Ezekiel, when, in the obstinate worship of their false gods, and the incorrigible apostasy of their hearts, they rejected His Theocratic
supremacy over them six hundred years before.

In the judicial blindness of their hearts, they refused to consider that it had never been covenanted
to them, that their Messiah should set up His temporal kingdom of unequalled earthly glory and exaltation so long as they continued in their sins, but
then only, when they should be converted from them.
In their judicial blindness, they altogether refused to
believe that they were a sinful and unbelieving nation. In their blind apostasy and blind expectation
of merely earthly state and splendor, an expectation
which honored not their Messiah, and exalted not
His glory, excepting in a merely earthly and human
sense, but their own worldly glory only; and in their
sinful and obstinate determination to realize and en-
joy the covenanted glories of the Messianic kingdom
without repentance and forgiveness of their sins;
they forfeited and lost both their Messiah's spiritual
and Davidic kingdom; or, if they did not wholly lose
them, they indefinitely postponed their covenanted
manifestation and glory, and doomed themselves
anew to the curses which Moses and the judicial
blindness which Isaiah had pronounced upon them,
and to stumble and be broken in pieces, throughout
the vast and weary and sorrowful round of their
judicial dispensation, upon the Rock, which, as the

original builders they thus obstinately and fatally refused.

What utterly inexcusable not less than fatal folly, to deny that our Saviour was their predicted Messiah! How plainly His primogenitive right to the vacant throne of David was established by the Jewish records, which their Rabbis could so well and readily interpret in all other respects! How clearly and indisputably, according to those records, did He unite in Himself the right of the posterity of David in both of its lines, at the time of His birth, to the indefeasible possession of the throne of David! According to these records, this right centered in our Saviour, both by the line of Solomon and by that of Nathan, each of whom were alike descended from David and Bathsheba, to whose posterity, in particular, the original grant had especially restricted the promise of an hereditary temporal kingdom. At the time of the Babylonian captivity, these lines were united in the person of Zorobabel, and at the birth of Christ they were united in the person of Christ; the right of Resa, one of the sons of Zorobabel, being transmitted to him through Eli and Mary, and the right of Abiud, another son of Zorobabel, through Joseph. Thus the indefeasible right of the posterity of David to the temporal throne of Israel, such as it had been covenanted to them forever by the promise of God before David had any posterity, became finally centered in the person of Jesus Christ; both in the natural sense as the first-born of Mary, and in the civil and legal sense as the first-born of Joseph. How perfectly coincident with this record, the announcement of the angel Gabriel to the virgin Mary, "Behold, thou shalt conceive in thy womb, and bring forth a son, and shalt call His name Jesus. He shall be great, and shall be called the Son of the Highest; and the Lord shall give unto Him the throne of His father David, and He shall reign over the house of Israel forever."

So also His divine claims as the King of grace, or
their spiritual Messiah, were no less clearly attested
by His innumerable miracles, than were His legal
claims as the King of Israel, or their temporal Messiah, by the Jewish records. But they despised and
rejected Him, putting Him to the base death of a
Roman slave, and invoking upon their own heads,
and upon the heads of their children, His innocent
blood. And there the self-invoked and bloody curse
has rested ever since, and will continue to rest, until,
red with its uncommon wrath, the covenants of the
divine wrath shall all be fulfilled upon them. Such
was the crowning iniquity, under the New-Testament
dispensation, of their judicial blindness, their judicial
condemnation and their judicial shame!

And what was the result of their rejection of their
Messiah? The parable of the wicked husbandmen
teaches us. In this, which, it will be remembered, is
one of the public and unexplained parables, our Saviour, having foretold His own crucifixion (within
three days afterwards), adds :—

"Did ye never read in the Scriptures, the stone which the
builders rejected, the same is become the head of the corner;
this is the Lord's doing, and it is marvellous in our eyes ?
Therefore I say unto you, The kingdom of God shall be
taken from you, and shall be given to a nation bringing forth
the fruits thereof. And whosoever shall fall on this stone
shall be broken; but on whomsoever it shall fall, it will grind
him to powder."

The nation here referred to does not mean, as is
sometimes loosely supposed, the Gentile nations in
distinction from the Jewish nation. In this the best
expositors are very generally agreed. Neither is it
meant that the kingdom of God, or the Messiah's
spiritual kingdom, should be taken from the Jewish
nation, and given to all nations indiscriminately, Jew
and Gentile alike, considered as one nation ; either
then, or at any time during the progress of the
present dispensation. The meaning is, as we hope
to explain, that the Messiah's spiritual kingdom

should be taken from the Jewish nation, considered
as the Jewish Church, Christ's only visible Church
on earth hitherto, but now hopelessly apostate, and
given, not, as might at first be supposed, to the professing Christian Church at large, under the present
Gospel dispensation, but to Christ's elect Church, the
ἔθνος ἅγιον, His chosen "remnant according to the
election of grace," chosen out of Jews and Gentiles
both ; chosen out of all nations, and all generations,
all kindreds and tribes and tongues, Jew and Greek,
Scythian and barbarian, bond and free. This is
Alford's exposition of this passage from Matthew,
and it appears to us to be Scriptural and sound.

Such, then, is the nation here referred to by our
Saviour. Such is the only nation that bringeth forth,
that ever has brought forth, that ever will bring forth,
fruit in its season. The allusion is not to any particular professing Church, or to the professing Church
at large, which is very far from bringing forth fruit
in its season, excepting so far only as it includes the
chosen remnant, the elect Church, the holy nation.
The Jewish nation, under the Old-Testament dispensation, was a professing Church, but it was as barren
and unfruitful as the fig-tree, which, in another of
our Saviour's public and unexplained parables, sym-
bolized it. But there was always a faithful remnant,
according to the foreknowledge of God, preserved in
it ; "a chosen generation," that belonged not in any
spiritual sense to the wicked and adulterous generation which composed the professing Jewish Church
at large ; "a royal priesthood," which, restricted not
to the tribe of Levi, offered up spiritual sacrifices
acceptable to God by the typified blood of their
coming Messiah ; seven thousand who worshiped
not at Dan and Bethel, and bowed not to Ashteroth
or Baal, or to any of "the hosts of heaven." This
holy nation ever existed, under the Old-Testament
dispensation, within the unholy Jewish nation at
large, and within the corrupt and apostate professing
Jewish Church at large. Preserved in the ark of God's

ancient and everlasting covenants of blessing, it out-rode all the storms of God's covenants of wrath under the Old-Testament dispensation, and, in its Jewish successors, will outride all the storms of the covenants of wrath under the New-Testament dispensation; greatly enlarged, however, by "the remnant according to the election of grace," which will be gathered out of the Gentile nations (Acts xv, 14), under the present dispensation; while on the other hand, the unbelieving and ungodly Gentile nations at large under the new dispensation, like the unbelieving and ungodly Jewish nation at large under the old, and the unbelieving and apostate professing Christian Church at large under the new dispensation, like the unbelieving and apostate professing Jewish Church at large under the old, will, in the end, and in like manner, be disowned and destroyed. In a word, and the unexplained parables, we believe, will show it, the history of the professing Jewish Church under the Old-Testament dispensation, is an exact type of what in the end will be the history of the professing Christian Church under the New-Testament dispensation. The proud and vain hopes of the Gentile nations, professing themselves Christian, and of the Gentile Church, professing itself Christian, will be as sorely disappointed and as ingloriously overthrown at the second coming of Israel's Messiah, as were those of the professing Jewish Church and nation at His first coming. He was wise who proclaimed, "The thing that hath been, it is that which shall be; and that which is done is that which shall be done: and there is no new thing under the sun."

But the chosen remnant always remains. It always has been preserved. It always will be preserved. Absolutely, they are a great multitude, a multitude which no man can number. But, relatively, as compared with the unbelieving world at large, whose prince and god Satan is, and will be, to the end of the dispensation, they are, as our Saviour calls them, "a little flock." They only are the holy nation. They

only bring forth fruits in their season. The professing Christian Church brings forth no fruit, excepting
so far only as this holy remnant are numbered among
its professors, precisely as the professing Jewish
Church brought forth fruit so far only as they were
members of that Church. The holy nation only, as
in the parable of the sower, brings forth some thirty,
and some sixty, and some an hundred fold. They
only, as in the parable of the tares, are the wheat
that will be gathered into the heavenly garners,
while the tares, that grow together with them till
the harvest, will be burned with unquenchable fire.
They only, as in the parable of the draw-net, are the
good fish that, when the net is drawn to the shore,
will be gathered into vessels, while the bad are cast
away. They only, as in the parables of the pounds
and the talents, will faithfully fulfil their several
trusts, and give a good account of their stewardship
when their absent Lord returns. They only, as in
the parable of the marriage of the king's son, will
sit down at the marriage-supper of the Lamb,
arrayed in their white robes. Their lamps only, as
in the parable of the ten virgins, will be found
trimmed and burning, when the cry is heard, " Behold the bridegroom cometh, go ye out to meet Him."
They only, as in the beautiful parable of the Song
which Solomon wrote in the best moments of his
life, are the virgin who dwelleth among the gardens,
who may treat her beloved coldly, as he stands at the
door and knocks, his head filled with the dew and
his locks with the drops of the morning, but who,
anon, becomes distressed for him, and calls after
him, and seeks for him among the gardens and the
bed of spices where he is gone down; she often for-
getting, but he never forgetful, His love never chang-
ing, He the highest of all the sons of men, the chiefest
among ten thousand, and the One altogether lovely.
They only will inherit, in their sevenfold spiritual
completeness, the blessed promises of the beatitudes.
Their names only are written from the foundation

of the world in the Book of Life of the slain Lamb. They only follow the Lamb whithersoever He goeth. They only are the sheep who know His voice and answer to His call. They only bear His reproach without the gates, loving not their lives, if need be, even unto death. Of them only is the holy army of the martyrs composed. They only, of those who profess the form of godliness, attest the power thereof. They only will hold fast till Christ comes, for "called and chosen and faithful" is their name. They only are strangers and pilgrims, sometimes almost losing their way amidst the storms and darkness, the allurements and perplexities and confusions, of a ruined and revolted world; having no continuing city here, but seeking one to come. They only, and not the professing Church (no mention whatever is made of that), are described in the Book of Revelation as bearing a faithful testimony to the very end of the dispensation, and in the midst of the judicial terrors of its closing scenes, against the overwhelming odds of the thronging powers of darkness, even though made war upon and overcome by them; overcome till He comes whose right it is to tread the guilty world in the wine-press of the fierceness and wrath of the Almighty God. They only, and those of them only who are of the seed of Abraham, inheriting at last God's faithful covenants, will reconstruct banished and shattered and down-trodden Israel, and build again her waste places, and build again the tabernacle of David which is fallen down, and build again the ruins thereof, and set it up; that the residue of men and all the Gentiles may seek after the Lord, till from the rising of the sun, even unto the going down thereof His name shall be great among them. Yes, they, they only, a thousand times be it said, are the holy nation, to whom the kingdom of God, Christ's spiritual kingdom, His precious vineyard, can in a just and legitimate, and strict and true, or literal, or spiritual sense be said to have been given, when it was taken from the apostate Jewish nation,

and apostate Jewish Church, and given unto them:
"Fear not, little flock, for it is your Father's good
pleasure to give you the kingdom."

The apostle Peter, in admonishing the infant
Church of its high calling, its privileges, its duties and its dangers, thus beautifully and propheti-
cally describes the elect and holy nation, as contrasted
with the world at large throughout the whole course
of the present dispensation, down to the second coming of our Saviour, or as the apostle styles it, "the
day of visitation."

"As new-born babes, desire the sincere milk of the word,
that ye may grow thereby; if so be ye have tasted that the
Lord is gracious, to whom coming, as unto a living stone,
disallowed indeed of men, but chosen of God, and precious;
ye also, as lively stones, are built up a spiritual house, a
holy priesthood, to offer up spiritual sacrifices acceptable to
God by Jesus Christ. Wherefore, also, it is contained in
the Scriptures, Behold, I lay in Zion a chief corner-stone,
elect, precious; and he that believeth in him shall not be
confounded. Unto you, therefore, which believe, he is
precious: but unto them which be disobedient, the stone
which the builders disallowed, the same is made the head of
the corner, and a stone of stumbling, and a rock of offense,
even to them which stumble at the word, being disobedient:
whereunto all they were appointed. But ye are a chosen
generation, a royal priesthood, a holy nation, a peculiar
people; that ye should show forth the praises of him who
called you out of darkness into his marvelous light. Dearly
beloved, I beseech you as strangers and pilgrims, abstain
from fleshly lusts, which war against the soul: having your
conversation honest among the Gentiles [the unconverted
world around you] : that whereas they speak against you as
evil doers, they may by your good works, which they shall
behold, glorify God in the day of visitation."

Not less beautifully, though less in its abstract
and spiritual, and more in its prophetico-historical
relations, has the apostle Paul described that portion
of the holy nation which consists of the Jewish
"election" only.

When the apostle wrote his Epistle to the Romans,

the curse of judicial blindness was resting upon
apostate Israel, and, in respect to the covenants of
blessing, the remnant of Israel according to the election of grace were the only representatives of the
nation that were left, the nation at large being "concluded in unbelief."

"I say then, hath God cast away his people ? God forbid.
For I also am an Israelite, of the seed of Abraham, of the
tribe of Benjamin. God hath not cast away his people
which he foreknew [that is, His elect remnant in the sense
above explained].   Wot ye not what the Scripture saith of
Elias ? how he maketh intercession to God against Israel,
saying, Lord, they have killed thy prophets, and digged
down thine altars ; and I am left alone, and they seek my
life.   But what saith the answer of God unto him ?   I have
reserved to myself seven thousand men, who have not bowed
the knee to the image of Baal. Even so then at this present
time, also, there is a remnant according to the election of
grace.   Israel [the unbelieving nation at large] hath not
obtained that which he seeketh for ; but the election hath
obtained it, and the rest were blinded."

The apostle tells us, directly afterwards, how long
Israel's judicial blindness will last.

"For I would not, brethren, that ye should be ignorant
of this mystery, lest ye should be wise in your own conceits,
that blindness in part is happened to Israel, *until the fullness
of the Gentiles be come in.*   And so all Israel shall be
saved : as it is written, There shall come out of Z on the
Deliverer, and shall turn away ungodliness from Jacob ; for
this is my covenant unto them, when I shall take away their
sins."

"*Until the fullness of the Gentiles be come in;*"
that is, until the fullness, or full complement, of
the Gentile elect shall be gathered in from the unbelieving Gentile nations; or, which is the same
thing, until the times of the Gentiles shall be fulfilled ; even as our Saviour said to His disciples,
" And they [Israel] shall fall by the edge of the
sword, and shall be led away captive into all nations,

and Jerusalem shall be trodden down of the Gentiles, until the times of the Gentiles shall be fulfilled."

This is the prophetic order. The events, however, are synchronous in their occurrence. The fullness of the Gentiles will come in. The full complement of "the remnant according to the election," of Christ's elect and invisible Church, of the holy nation, being gathered in and made up from among the unbelieving nations, the dispensation will end. The times of the Gentiles will be fulfilled. The dispensation of unbelief will end. The dispensation, or, rather, the ages of faith, will begin. Israel's blindness will be removed. Israel's Messiah will come again, and will not be rejected. "The Spirit of grace and of supplications" will be poured out upon the house of Israel. All the tribes of the land will "look upon Him whom they have pierced," when "in that day His feet shall stand upon the Mount of Olives," and will mourn because of their past rejection of Him, and because of all their sins and uncleanness, with great and unparalleled mourning; even as one mourneth for his only son and is in bitterness for his first-born. God "will take away their sins," and "will cast their sins into the depths of the sea," and will bestow upon them, in full fruition, all the blessings of all His covenants of blessing with them. The holy seed, or holy remnant of Israel, will swell into stately national proportions, a new Israel, regenerate, re-created, "born in a day," and, according to the covenant, "set on high above all the nations of the earth." David will never again want a man to sit upon his now vacant throne to the end of the dispensations which are revealed. Christ will sit and reign thereon through all the millennial years, alike as the King of glory, the King of David, and the King of grace, in the manifested and triumphant glory both of temporal and spiritual sovereignty, to the utmost limit of the record of the ages which are revealed; till time ends, and eternity begins.

Thus much concerning the *Jewish* "remnant ac-

cording to the election of grace," and the prophetic
future which awaits them.   Concerning the *Gentile*
"remnant according to the election of grace," and
the future which also awaits them, equally clear testimony is not wanting.

The apostle James speaks expressly (Acts xv,
14, etc.) of this holy Gentile remnant, as gathered
out of the unbelieving Gentile nations under the present Gospel dispensation.   The stand-point, as it will
be observed, from which he takes his survey, is the
close of the next, or millennial, dispensation.

"Simeon [Simon Peter] hath declared how God at the
first [at the commencement of the Gospel dispensation, and
upon the rejection by Israel of her Messiah] did visit the
Gentiles, [not *to convert* them, but] to take out of them a
people for his name.   And to this agree the words of the
prophet ; as it is written, after this [after the close of the
Gospel dispensation, and at the commencement of the next,
or millennial, dispensation] *I will return*, and will build
again the tabernacle of David, which is fallen down, and I
will build again the ruins thereof, and I will set it up: that
the residue of men may seek after the Lord, and all the
Gentiles, upon whom my name is called, saith the Lord,
who doeth all these things."

The apostle's allusion in this passage is evidently
to the future exaltation and glory of the Jewish
nation in the next, or millennial, dispensation ; and
to the universal in-gathering into the elect and holy
nation, or spiritual Israel, under that dispensation,
of the remaining Gentiles of the earth ; in accordance with the covenant of God with Abraham that,
in its fulfilment, not Israel alone, but " all the families of the earth, should be blessed."   Meanwhile the
guilty world will roll on in its sins, until its last
revolution, under the present dispensation, is complete.

The guilty and unbelieving Jewish nation—with
its invincible tenacity and individuality of life; its vast
resources of silver and gold ; its universal solvency
in the midst of universal insolvency; its undecaying

intellectual manhood and incomparable learning; its
mighty and resistless hold upon the political des-
tinies of the very nations that tread it down; its
ever-restless wanderings into all the uttermost re-
gions of the earth; its curious eternal countenance,
never varying from its one eternal type, whether as
seen in the tombs of Babylon, the pyramids of Egypt,
on the entablatures of Nineveh, or in the highest
seats of European learning, and the proudest coun-
cils of European state; with its judicial blindness
and reserve; always rejecting its Messiah; always re-
sisting the Holy Ghost (" as your fathers did, so do
ye"); always, according to the prophetic command
of our Saviour, filling up the measure of its fathers;
always, like the bush of their own Horeb, in the
flames of the Divine wrath, but never consumed;
always dismantled and dismembered, outcast and
dispersed and trodden-down—will roll on in its sins,
until overwhelmed at last by the fiery waves of its
greatest and last tribulation, and the times of the
Gentiles are fulfilled.

So also, on the other hand, the guilty and
unbelieving Gentile nations—who, as nations,
are of *no recorded account* in the prophetic
Scriptures, either under Israel's probationary or
judicial dispensation, except as Israel's oppressors only—with their Christian professions and
assumptions; their mighty races and nationalities,
striding through the world as Nebuchadnezzar strode
through his halls, and looking complacently forth
upon the great Babylons they have built by the might
of their power, and for the honor of their majesty;
with their stately and imposing civilizations; their
combined and successful expositions of utmost
human splendor and utmost human endeavor;
their social refinements and accomplishments
and ameliorations; their grand but unsuccessful,
and so often anarchical attempts to govern themselves apart from God and in alienation from Him;
their " strong delusion;" their audacious and infatu-

ated self-confidence and egotism and self-conceit, and
their bankrupt exchequers—will roll on, in judicial
unconsciousness of their fate, to their common ruin,·
their utter confusion and dismay, their complete and
final and judicial overthrow; melting at last, like Pros-
peros' spirits, from their intoxicated revels,

> " *   *   into air, into thin air,
> And like the baseless fabric of a vision,
>   *   *   *   *   *   *
> An insubstantial pageant faded, dissolve,
> Nor leave a rack behind."

We do not speak of the Gentile nations, or great
world-powers of the Gentiles, as being, or ever becoming, apostate, in the sense in which Israel is apostate. They have never owned or recognized Jehovah
as ruling over the affairs of men, in the sense in which
Israel has, in time past, so owned and recognized
Him ; and they cannot therefore apostatize from Jehovah, in the sense in which Israel has apostatized
from Him. So also, on the other hand, has God
never owned or recognized the Gentile nations, in the
sense in which He has owned and recognized Israel,
nor made covenants with them, as He has made covenants with Israel. But their guilt and delusion is
not therefore any less, but only greater, and their
doom will be only more sudden and terrible, in that
they have not so owned and recognized Him. There
was the profoundest historic truth, reaching into all
the coming Jewish and Gentile generations, in the
prayer of the children of Israel by the waters of
Babylon ; "Return for thy servant's sake, the tribes
of thine inheritance. The people of thy holiness have
possessed it but a little while ; our adversaries have
trodden down thy sanctuary. We are *thine ;* thou
never barest rule over them ; they were not called by
thy name."

The unbelieving Gentile nations, and we refer
more particularly to those great world-powers which
have the most conspicuous prophetic record as the

3

oppressors of Israel; to those which, in their prophetic and collective unity, are represented by Nebuchadnezzar's image; to Babylon, Persia, Greece
and Rome, and the present sovereignties into which
the Roman empire was divided; cannot, with any
Scriptural propriety, now or ever, be called apostate
nations. They have had no High and Holy One, in
the sense that Israel had, to apostatize or fall away
from. They have never belonged to God. God has
never owned them as His people. They have only
been known to Him as the oppressors of His people,
treading them down, and treading down His sanctuary between the seas in the glorious holy mountain; and prophecy only recognizes in them the
oppressors and treaders-down of Israel, until their
own evil times shall be fulfilled. God never bore
rule over them. They were never called by His
name. They are only known to prophecy, to
the Old Testament and to the New, in the
broad and generalized sense of "the kingdoms of
this world," whose prince and god is Satan; to
which kingdoms "the kingdom of God," or
"kingdom of heaven," as it is so constantly called
by our Saviour, and especially in His unexplained
parables, is, with such antithetical emphasis, opposed;
and if Israel, with her covenants, is scarcely saved,
where will the great unbelieving and anti-Christian
world-powers appear, when God makes up His account
and has His final controversy with "the nations?"

"The gods of the nations are idols." They can
only apostatize from their own chosen gods, which
alas! "the sure word of prophecy" assures us
they never will, certainly until the end of their own
times, under the present dispensation; when, but not
till then, "the kingdoms of this world and the glory
of them," with which Satan tempted Christ in vain,
"shall become the sovereignty of our Lord and of His
Christ, and He shall reign for ever and ever." They
may in their dreams baptize, in solemn mockery, with
their own unholy baptism, the stately image which

Nebuchadnezzar saw in his dream, and call it Christendom, and call themselves Christian nations, Christian legs of iron, and Christian feet and toes of iron mixed with miry clay, but, for all that, God will not be mocked. The interpretation of the dream is sure. God's destroying vengeance is sure. "In the days of these kings shall the God of heaven set up a kingdom which shall never be destroyed; and the kingdom shall not be left to other people, but it shall break in pieces and consume all these kingdoms, and it shall stand forever." The unbelieving "kingdoms of the world" may profess Christianity, but they will not apostatize from their own chosen gods; may array themselves in the livery of the angels of light, and seek to be as gods, as Satan promised them they should be, but they will not apostatize. They may profess, and seek to dignify themselves by the name of, Christianity, but professing Christianity is not vital Christianity. To profess Christianity is not to be born again. The professing Christian Church may, like the professing Jewish Church, apostatize; it will apostatize; but *they* will not apostatize from *their* gods.

This great disparity, this mighty antagonism, of moral forces—a little remnant, constituting the elect and holy nation on the one hand, the great mass of mankind, or, as the apostle says, "the whole world lying in wickedness," on the other; the rightful but rejected Sovereign of the world on the one hand, its usurping, but preferred and accepted sovereign on the other; the powers of light on the one hand, the powers of darkness on the other; the Great Deliverer on the one hand, the great destroyer on the other; Christ on the one hand, antichrists many, to the final Antichrist on the other, has always existed, and now exists, and will continue to exist, until the present evil dispensation is ended, or, which is the same thing, so long as the New-Testament revelation truly represents the moral character and condition of mankind, is applicable to it, and intended for it.

Next in importance to the holy nation, in the discussion of our theme, is the prophetic history of the Jewish nation, past, present and to come, as recorded in the prophetic Scriptures.

This nation demands our special attention, not only because they are God's chosen and peculiar people; the central people of the earth in His plan of moral government; towards whom the course of His holy providence among the affairs of men always tends, and around whom all history revolves; not only because they are the seed, through whom alone God has appointed that all the nations of the earth shall ultimately be blessed, and without whose intervention and ultimate conversion, according to His appointed method, and in His Own appointed way, the nations of the Gentiles have no promised ground of hope; and not only because they have been, and are still to be, more severely chastised in the heat of His great anger, and in the furnace of His great wrath, than any other nation; and because they are to be correspondingly exalted, when, in wrath remembering mercy, He shall redeem His covenants with their fathers, and avenge Himself upon their foes, and bring them to repentance, and forgive their sins, and set them on high in honor and blessing above all the nations of the earth; but because also, which more especially concerns our present theme, it was to them that the prophetic parables of our Saviour were personally addressed, and for reasons, as our Saviour Himself informs us (Matt. xiii, 10–16), especially adapted to the circumstances of their moral condition, or, rather, to their total want of right moral understanding, to the judicial hardness and insensibility of their hearts, at the time when they were spoken.

In our proposed review of Israel's prophetic history, we shall, if we mistake not, arrive at the following results or conclusions:—

1. That the prophetic history of Israel includes the whole of three distinct dispensations, or αἰῶνες;

namely, the past or Mosaic, the present or Christian, and the future, or millennial.

2. That the particular dispensation referred to in any particular prophecy. or class of prophecies, is, as a general rule, clearly distinguishable.

3. We shall arrive at a clear Scriptural knowledge of the moral condition of the Jewish nation, at the conjunction, τα τέλη τῶν αἰώνων, of these several dispensations: at the conjunction, first, of the Mosaic and Christian dispensations, when parabolic prophecy, as a distinct and customary form of prophecy, began first to be employed; and at the conjunction, secondly, of the Christian and millennial dispensations, when the parabolic and all other prophetic judgments against Israel will be fulfilled; whenceforward millennial prophecy opens the glorious vista of Israel's millennial future to our view; in which glory " the residue of the Gentiles," according to the promise, will share.

4. We shall arrive at equally clear proof that the past, or Mosaic, dispensation was to Israel, as a nation, a disciplinary, or probationary, dispensation; that the present, or Christian, dispensation is to Israel a judicial, or penal, as it is to the Gentile nations a probationary, dispensation; Israel remaining, according to the covenants of wrath, in her sins and judicial blindness until its close; and that the future, or millennial, dispensation will be to Israel a dispensation of everlasting peace and repose, and honor and blessing, and glory and exaltation, " above all the nations of the earth," according to the covenants of blessing; when, but not till then, the covenants which God sware unto Abraham, and Isaac, and Jacob, that in their seed all the nations of the earth should be blessed, shall be gloriously fulfilled; when, but not till then, the Gentile nations, their proud spirit humbled, and their proud Babels fallen, shall not only acknowledge and proclaim that Israel is the seed which the Lord hath blessed, but shall hasten to her light and to the brightness of her rising with

songs and everlasting joy, bringing their tribute from afar, and their offerings from the ends of the earth ; when, but not till then, the Theocracy which Israel forfeited by her sins, and of which, in the multitude of her iniquities and transgressions, she was unworthy, shall be gloriously restored, and, the warfare of the elect Church militant and the predicted overturning and overturning and overturning of the unbelieving nations being ended, the Root and Offspring of David, the Bright and Morning Star, shall arise and shine, and sit upon the throne of His father David in the manifested, triumphant and covenanted glory both of His Davidic and spiritual kingdom, and reign forever and ever.

. Such is the divine order of the dispensations, probationary, judicial, and millennial; such the appointed method of God's holy government, and the appointed course of God's holy providence, by which He will at last restore apostate Israel, and, through Israel, all mankind to their original likeness and their original allegiance to Himself. Such is the prophetic record ; and whosoever leaves it out of account, or adds to it, or takes from it, in dealing with the secret, but, to the eye of faith, revealed problems of man's spiritual being and destiny, or seeks by any method of man's wisdom, to climb up some other way to their solution, whether Church or State be the theme of his discourse, at the least that can be said, darkens counsel by words without knowledge. But the record is before us. Let it speak for itself.

The whole future of Israel's prophetic history, with its interwoven prophetic history of the Gentile nations as her oppressors, was foretold, in outline, by Moses, the founder of the nation and its prophet without a peer (Deut. xxxiv, 10), when, at the close of their wanderings in the wilderness, they were about to enter into the land, whither, for forty weary and guilty years, they had been going to possess it. These prophecies (Deut. xxviii–xxx), including the dying ode of Moses, were his parting message, his last will

and testament, to the sinful and erring nation, the
vox cycnea of the departing seer. They are a prophetic mirror, revealing in general and, sometimes,
particular outline, the whole future history of the
nation, down to the end of the dispensations which
are revealed; down to that utmost limit of time, beyond which inspired prophecy, in respect to man's
earthly condition and estate, stretches not its ken;
down to that utmost limit of time, where the unrevealed dispensations begin, where the Divine Revelation merges itself in those of ages of ages, those
αἰῶνες τῶν αἰώνων, by which in the Holy Scriptures
the eternity of God is so often described. The
alternatives of blessing and cursing, presented to
the nation by these prophecies, were made to stand
out in impending relief, even as Ebal, the mount of
cursing, and Gerizim, the mount of blessing, then
stood before their natural eyes. The whole future
history of Israel, its judicial blindness in the nearer
future, and its final conversion and exaltation in the
more remote, was wrapped up in these prophecies, as
the mighty oak is wrapped up in the little acorn we
tread beneath our feet. However familiar our readers
may be with these prophecies, we hope they will re-
peruse the selections we make from them, for the sake
of their importance to our discussion.

" And it shall come to pass, if thou shalt hearken
diligently unto the voice of the Lord thy God, to observe and to do all his commandments which I command thee this day, that the Lord thy God will set
thee on high above all the nations of the earth; and
all these blessings shall come on thee, and overtake
thee, if thou shalt hearken unto the voice of the Lord
thy God. Blessed shalt thou be in the city, and
blessed shalt thou be in the field. Blessed shalt
the fruit of thy body, and the fruit of thy ground,
and the fruit of thy cattle, the increase of thy kine,
and the flocks of thy sheep. Blessed shall be thy
basket and thy store. Blessed shalt thou be when
thou comest in, and blessed shalt thou be when

thou goest out. The Lord shall cause thine enemies
that rise up against thee to be smitten before thy
face; they shall come out against thee one way, and
flee before thee seven ways. The Lord shall command the blessing upon thee in thy storehouse, and
in all that thou settest thine hand unto; and he shall
bless thee in the land the Lord thy God giveth thee.
The Lord shall establish thee a holy people unto himself, as he hath sworn unto thee, if thou shalt keep
the commandments of the Lord thy God, and walk
in his ways; and all people of the earth shall see that
thou art called by the name of the Lord; and they
shall be afraid of thee. And the Lord shall make
thee plenteous in goods, in the fruit of thy body, and
in the fruit of thy cattle, and in the fruit of thy
ground, in the land which the Lord sware unto thy
fathers to give thee. The Lord shalt open unto thee
his good treasure, the heaven to give thee rain into
thy land in his season, and to bless all the work of
thine hand; and thou shalt lend unto many nations,
and thou shalt not borrow. And the Lord shall
make thee the head, and not the tail; and thou shalt
be above only, and thou shalt not be beneath; if that
thou hearken unto the commandments of the Lord
thy God, which I command thee this day, to observe
and to do them, and shalt not go aside from any of
the words which I command thee this day, to the
right hand, or to the left, to go after other gods to
serve them.

" But it shall come to pass, if thou will not hearken
unto the voice of the Lord thy God, to observe to do
all his commandments and his statutes which I command thee this day; that all these curses shall come
upon thee, and overtake thee. Cursed shalt thou be
in the city, and cursed shalt thou be in the field.
Cursed shalt be thy basket and thy store. Cursed
shall be the fruit of thy body, and the fruit of thy
land, the increase of thy kine, and the flocks of thy
sheep. Cursed shalt thou be when thou comest in,
and cursed shalt thou be when thou goest out. The

Lord shall send upon thee cursing, vexation, and rebuke, in all that thou settest thine hand unto for to do, until thou be destroyed, and until thou perish quickly; because of the wickedness of thy doings, whereby thou hast forsaken me. The Lord shall make the pestilence cleave unto thee, until he hath consumed thee from off the land, whither thou goest to possess it. The Lord shall smite thee with a consumption, and with a fever, and with an inflammation, and with an extreme burning, and with the sword, and with blasting, and with mildew; and they shall pursue thee until thou perish. And thy heaven which is over thy head shall be brass, and the earth that is under thee shall be iron. The Lord shall make the rain of thy land powder and dust; from heaven shall it come down upon thee, till thou be destroyed. The Lord shall cause thee to be smitten before thine enemies; thou shalt go out one way against them, and flee seven ways before them; and shalt be removed into all the kingdoms of the earth. The Lord shall smite thee with madness, and with blindness, and with astonishment of heart; and thou shalt grope at noon-day, as the blind gropeth in darkness, and thou shalt not prosper in thy ways; and thou shalt be only oppressed and spoiled evermore, and no man shall save thee; thou shalt be only oppressed and crushed alway. And thou shalt become an astonishment, a proverb, and a byword among all nations whither the Lord shall lead thee. The stranger that is within thee shall get up above thee very high, and thou shalt come down very low. He shall be the head, and thou shalt be the tail. Thou shalt serve thine enemies, which the Lord shall send against thee, in hunger, and in thirst, and in nakedness, and in want of all things, and he shall put a yoke of iron upon thy neck, until he have destroyed thee. The Lord shall bring a nation against thee from far, from the end of the earth, as swift as the eagle flieth; a nation whose tongue thou shalt not understand; a nation of fierce countenance, which

4

shall not regard the person of the old, nor show favor
to the young: and he shall eat the fruit of thy cattle,
and the fruit of thy land, until thou be destroyed!
which also shall not leave thee either corn, or oil, or
the increase of thy kine, or flocks of thy sheep, until
he have destroyed thee. And he shall besiege thee
in all thy gates, until thy high and fenced walls come
down, wherein thou trustedst, throughout all thy
land; and he shall besiege thee in all thy gates
throughout all thy land, which the Lord thy God
hath given thee. And thou shalt eat the fruit of
thine own body, the flesh of thy sons and of thy
daughters, which the Lord thy God hath given thee,
in the siege, and in the straitness, wherewith thine
enemies shall distress thee. And ye shall be
plucked from off the land whither thou goest to
possess it: and the Lord shall scatter thee among
all people, from the one end of the earth even unto
the other; and among these nations shalt thou find
no ease, neither shall the sole of thy foot have rest:
but the Lord shall give thee there a trembling heart,
and failing of eyes, and sorrow of mind, and thy life
shall hang in doubt before thee."

We ask the attention of our readers, especially, to
the incontestably literal character of these predictions. They were all prophecy then. They are all
accomplished facts and actual history now. All the
world knows it by heart. Their literal fulfilment in
the past is attested by eye-witnesses in records without number, written without concert, and universally
harmonious. The now occurring literal fulfilment of
many of them is but a repetition of their literal fulfilment in the past, and a faithful record in advance
of their no less literal fulfilment in the future, "till
all shall be fulfilled;" or, in other words of our Saviour, "until the times of the Gentiles shall be fulfilled." There is not a single prediction, in this long
catalogue of prophecies, that has not been justified by
the event, and, in the case of the most of them, over
and over again.

Look, for instance, at the prediction of the destruction of Jerusalem by the Romans—to whom expositors and historians for the most part agree, that the "nation of fierce countenance" refers—which took place more than fifteen hundred years after the prediction was uttered. Where, in the pages of any historian, will you find a more truthful, or more graphic and vivid account of its actual, detailed and quivering horrors, than in these few words of Moses? where a description so terrible, and yet so literally truthful, of Israel's whole suffering future ever since; uttered by Moses before one of the prophetic acts of disobedience had been committed, or one of the prophetic judgments had been inflicted, or one of the prophetic woes had been endured, which these prophecies with such wonderful accuracy foretell? No uninspired historian of the past ever described with more faithful and literal exactness what has happened, than this inspired prophet foretold what would happen, never failing of the exact fact, as all history confirms, in so much as a single particular. The future was even clearer to his eye, though sweeping the vast and unrevealed future of other dispensations than his own, than the past can be to ours, though confined to much narrower fields. His rapt and unclouded vision could not err. Our clouded and uninspired vision, even with the best lights of history before us, often errs.

What a commentary upon the wickedness and perverseness of the nation, then just entering, under such glorious auspices, and under the guidance of such a heaven-inspired leader, upon its early manhood, was the necessity of these predictions of the consequences of its sins—always the last resort with the hopelessly incorrigible—as if, indeed, it would surely be guilty of them! Already do we seem to see the thick darkness of the judicial blindness, pronounced upon them seven hundred and fifty years afterwards, settling down with its baleful shadows over their foolish hearts.

And yet Moses, spanning the mighty arch of the coming dispensations, foresaw, through the faith and endurance of a chosen and holy remnant, which would always be preserved, the possible recovery and salvation of the nation at last; when, as another prophet foretells, they shall, at His second coming, behold their King in His terror and His beauty, and acknowledge Him, even in the latter days, as their bleeding but victorious Messiah. Five times in the dying ode of Moses (Delitzsch calls our attention to the number) is Christ referred to as the Rock of Israel; the Rock alike of her vengeance and of her salvation; the Rock upon which she will continue to fall and be broken in pieces, until her evil course is run; the Rock which will then fall upon her Gentile foes and grind them to powder; the Rock, however, in which she will hide herself at last. How beautiful the symbol, borrowed from the granite cliffs of Sinai; descending through the wanderings of the children of Israel in the wilderness; through the evil hours of their probationary, and the now far-spent night of their judicial dispensation; through the wrecks of their own and so many other buried empires; through the psalms and hymns of so many generations! the spiritual beauty and consolation of which has been so sweetly caught and breathed forth by one of our Christian poets:—

"Rock of ages cleft for me,
Let me hide myself in thee;" etc.

In passing from Moses to Isaiah, who stands midway between Moses and Christ, we approach a new era or dispensation in the prophetic history of Israel. Her probationary dispensation is about to end, and a long and dark and dreary night of rayless gloom is about to settle down upon the guilty nation; a night upon which no day-star will arise, to chase away its heaviness and anguish, until the close of another dispensation, of the present Gentile dispensation, and the coming-in of Israel's millennial dispensation.

It is the night of Israel's judicial blindness, judicial condemnation and judicial shame.

The prophecies of Moses, which we have cited, introduced, or completed the introduction, of a probationary dispensation to Israel. Accordingly, as has been seen, they were expressed in an alternative form. An alternative of blessing on the one hand, and of cursing on the other, was presented to the nation. An open choice was before her. Do this, and all the blessings of the covenants shall be yours. Do that, and they shall all be taken from you.

Notwithstanding these prophecies of Moses were thus probationary in their aspect and character, they were yet full of apprehension, lest Israel should reject the offered blessing, and choose the offered curse; and the apprehension was justified by the event. She did choose the offered curse, and she is now, under the prophetic mission of Isaiah, about to reap the judicial consequences of her evil choice. Since the time of Moses, she had been blessed with seasons of great national prosperity and splendor. Nevertheless she heaped rebellion upon rebellion, and apostasy upon apostasy, until now, at last, nearly all the prophetic judgments enumerated by Moses had come upon her and overtaken her, and were about to utterly destroy her national independence, and annihilate her national glory, until all things written in the law should be fulfilled upon her, and the bitter cup of the self-chosen curse should be drained to its dregs.

Hitherto, even in all her sins, Israel, as a nation, had leaned, or professed to lean, upon the arm of Jehovah alone. But now, under Ahaz, the kingdom of Judah (unmindful of the calamities which had come upon her sister kingdom of Israel, for casting of Jehovah, and calling in the aid of Egypt) called in herself, in like manner, against her sister kingdom, the aid of Assyria, and from that hour Jehovah was cast off by her; and Jehovah, in turn, cast her off, and delivered her over to her enemies.

In that hour she forged the first link in the chain of
her Assyrian oppression, in that chain of oppression,
which, beginning with Babylon, ended not with
Rome, nor will end, until all that is written
against the ungodly nation by these two great universal prophets of Israel, Moses and Isaiah, shall be
fulfilled upon her. From the hour that Israel, irreso-
lutely yielding to every temptation of idolatry,
melted her golden ear-rings into a golden calf in the
wilderness, and her incensed leader brake in pieces
the tables of stone, on which was inscribed, in the
hand-writing of Jehovah, first of all, "Thou shalt
have no other Gods before Me," down to the time
when Ahaz despoiled the temple of the Lord of its
silver and gold for a present to the king of Assyria,
and set up the worship of Molech, the savage god
of the Ammonites, upon the heights of Olivet and
under the very walls of Jerusalem, Israel's whole
career, especially since the last days of Solomon,
had been one of almost unceasing rebellion and idolatry.

What crowning sin, what crowning act of guilt,
could she now commit, when she had thus utterly cast
off the Most High God of Israel, in Whom alone her
whole national life and being had consisted hitherto,
to render her apostasy more complete, in thought, or
word, or deed? If this sin was not sufficient to call
down upon her the judicial wrath of heaven, what
sin would be sufficient to call it down? If she
merited not judicial condemnation now, when would
she merit it? True, if she now rejected and cast off
God the Father, she might, as she did, after another
seven hundred and fifty years, reject and cast off God
the Son, and God the Spirit, as she also did. But
this would be no new offense, but only a repetition of
the same offense against the same eternal and triune
Godhead, and therefore no reason why her judicial
sentence for the original offense should be postponed.
How otherwise than by her judicial condemnation
now, could the Divine justice, according even to the

most ordinary and limited ideas of human justice, be vindicated and maintained? How otherwise could any government, or theory of government, human or divine, stand for a single hour? No! for a period longer than the lifetime of any other nation before or since, a period of nearly a thousand years, Israel had been put upon her probation, and her probation had now proved a failure. Every recourse of, the divine goodness and every chastisement of the divine wrath had been exhausted upon her in vain. No nation had ever enjoyed opportunities so exalted. No nation had ever thrown them so entirely away. The foundations of no nation were ever laid on such glorious and indestructible covenants. No nation was ever established and upheld by such almighty power; with the infinite fulness of God pledged beforehand to supply all its human needs and deficiencies. No nation was ever regulated and guided in its whole national life and being and career by such infinite wisdom, or watched over in such infinite love, or borne with in its sins so tenderly or so long, or with a compassion so divine, or forgiven so many times: the wrath of God wrestled down for it by the heroic Jacob in advance; God dwelling ever in it in spite of its sins, and walking in it, and a God unto it as He was not God of any other people, that they might be to Him His people above all the people of the earth; their land the most favored of all lands, in respect to the independence of its natural position, (yet standing midway in the highway of the continents) its beauty of configuration, and the various and teeming fruitfulness of its soil; with no arm of flesh, but with Jehovah's almighty arm, to lean upon. But, alas! she yielded to the great adversary of Jehovah in His holy government over a fallen world, and fell. She had now, when Ahaz reigned and Isaiah prophesied, utterly cast off Jehovah. He had never ceased to call to her. She had never ceased to refuse. He had never ceased to stretch out His hand to her. She had never ceased to disregard it. There was no other god that she would not have before the most High God of Israel, the one ever-living and true God. And thus, by her own mad and suicidal folly, she put an end to her probation; and nothing now remains but to render the verdict, and pass the sentence of a holy and offended God upon her. ·

It is at this point, strictly speaking, that Israel's probationary dispensation ends, and her judicial dispensation begins; though we have before spoken of these dispensations, in their relations to Israel, in somewhat more general terms. Up to this point Israel's past history had been the history of a probationary dispensation. From this point we enter upon, and are to contemplate only, her judicial dispensation, until, through the faith and endurance of the holy remnant, she reaches, at the close of her judicial, her millennial, dispensation. Accordingly we find that from this point onward, the predictions of the prophets of Israel no longer assume a probationary aspect and character; presenting to the nation an alternative of blessing on the one hand, and of cursing on the other; but that they are *judicial only*, whenever they refer to any point or period of time *preceding* the close of her judicial, and the commencement of her millennial, dispensation; and *millennial only*, when they relate to a *subsequent* period of time; the second advent of her Messiah constituting, as we shall presently see, the boundary between the two dispensations.

Henceforward, prophecy, so far as it relates to actual events and results in Israel's future history, no longer expresses itself in an alternative, but only in the most absolute form, and in the most absolute terms. It no longer contemplates any possible contingency, or any doubtful and uncertain results, in respect to the future moral character and conduct of the nation. The guilty nation has made its choice, and its choice has been accepted, sealed and registered against it in the courts of heaven, and has assumed all the force and authority of a divine de-

cree. Henceforward, it is the judicial wrath of God
only that awaits her, and is predicted against her,
until she reaches the end of her present judicial dispensation. Of this character are all the prophecies
of Isaiah, and Jeremiah, and Ezekiel, and Daniel,
and of all the minor and later prophets, which relate
to Israel under her present judicial dispensation. Of
this character are all the prophecies of our Saviour,
which relate to the future moral history of the nation,
including His public and unexplained parables, which
are thus not prophetic only, but judicially prophetic
also. Thus, for example, our Saviour expressed himself in clearly judicial terms, and anticipated no pos-
sibly contingent or conditional, or twofold, or alternative results, when, in His last public discourse,
He gave to the guilty nation the prophetic command,
" Fill ye up then the measure of your fathers ; ye ser-
pents, ye generation of vipers, how can ye escape
the damnation of hell?" or when He no less pro-
phetically declared to the guilty nation, " Ye shall fall
by the edge of the sword, and shall be led away captive into all nations ; and Jerusalem shall be trodden
down of the Gentiles, until the times of the Gentiles
be fulfilled."

It was Moses who inaugurated the era, or dispensation, of probationary prophecy. It was Isaiah, the
statesman-like and fiery prophet of Jerusalem, with
whom the era of probationary prophecy ended, and
the dispensation of judicial prophecy began. There
is not to be found a prophecy in Isaiah, relating to
the actual future of Israel's history, that is susceptible of an alternative construction or application; that
is not clearly and absolutely either *judicial* in its
character on the one hand, or *millennial* in its character on the other, according to the particular dispensation referred to, or described. Isaiah, next to
Moses, is the universal prophet of Israel. His prophecies embrace the nation in all its tribes, and all its
generations, and in both of its coming dispensations.
He is the great prophet of Israel outcast and dis-

persed, and of Israel restored; of Israel's present
shame, and of Israel's future glory; of Israel trodden-
down, and of Israel lifted up. As we have already
said, these two classes of prophecy can always be
clearly distinguished from one another.

But especially do we love to contemplate Isaiah
as the prophet, pre-eminently, of Israel's millennium,
and through Israel, of the millennium of all mankind.
Indeed, he is the prophet, especially, as his name in
the Hebrew imports, of "Israel's salvation." There
is nothing in inspired prophecy that transcends in
touching beauty, or in lofty splendor, the millennial
visions of Isaiah:

> "From harmony to harmony.
> Through all the compass of the notes they run."

Of such and so great consequence to the moral
and spiritual destiny of Israel, and, through Israel,
of all mankind, was the terrible apostasy and fall of
this ancient, and sacred, and covenanted, but unfaith-
ful nation! Thus it has always been, and always will
be; with nations as with individuals; and Israel is
the great example. A nation is simply a name which
a collection of individuals agree with common con-
sent to assume: and what is there in a name, be it
Jew or Gentile, Greek or Roman, European or
American, that can change the moral relations and
responsibilities of man to his Creator, or lessen his
personal accountability? Can any number of individuals, by binding themselves together into a
nation, however skillfully and well they may
strengthen the cords, and refine and perfect the
organism, and consolidate the national unity and
individuality, and extend the national resources,
and foster the national pride, and heighten the
national prestige, that cement their common union,
and bind them together as one man—all which was
true of the Jewish nation; and has, at one time or
another, been true of all the great nations of the
earth—thus escape their individual accountability,
either singly, or as a people, to an injured and

offended God; or escape, if deserved, His judicial
wrath? Let condemned and down-trodden Israel
answer. Let the still crumbling ruins of Babylon
and Persia and Greece and Rome swell the mournful
echo. And why shall the present or future sovereignties of the earth return a less sad response?
We know from prophecies, which we shall presently
cite, that they will not.

In brief, God's method is simply this. He leaves
man to his own free and unrestrained moral choice;
to choose what course of moral conduct he will;
placing before him in His holy Word and in the
history of His holy providence the just, legitimate
and certain consequences of his acts, accordingly as
he elects and pursues one course of moral conduct or
another. If he elects and pursues a sinful course of
conduct, and hardens himself in guilt, and steels himself against repentance, and shuts his eyes, and his
ears, and his heart to every method which reason, and
persuasion, and judgment, and mercy can devise and
interpose, to turn him from his evil ways—all which
was true of sinful and guilty Israel in her relations
to her Heavenly Father, and in the relations of her
Heavenly Father to her—the loving will of God towards him becomes at length the wrathful will of
God, into which His loving will always changes, when
obstinately and incorrigibly resisted. Then ensues
the sentence of judicial blindness. Then, the self-
hardened sinner becomes the judicially-condemned
criminal. Then, the judicial and peremptory wrath
of God supervenes to deliver him over to the just
consequences of his own acts, his own self-chosen
conduct: to believe to his utter ruin and confusion,
the miserable lies with which the devil has cheated
him, and with which he has cheated himself; and bars
the door of repentance against him, which he has first
closed against himself.

Such was guilty Israel, when, more than twenty-
six hundred years ago, the sentence of judicial blindness, which her prophets had invoked and foretold,

was passed upon her. Such has guilty Israel been
ever since, abandoned alike of God and man. Thus
does sin bring upon itself its own punishment, which
is the wrath of God excited by it. With what heavenly pathos did our Saviour, the last time that He
wept over Jerusalem in the presence of His disciples,
alluding to the then and still existing execution of
the fearful sentence of Israel's judicial blindness, with
which He would not interfere, however much He
yearned to open their eyes, exclaim: " If thou hadst
known, even thou, at least in this thy day, the things
which belong unto thy peace! but now they are hid
from thy eyes."

But who by searching can find out the great mystery of Israel's judicial blindness? We can do little
more than recite the great fact itself as we find it recorded, and such other Scripture testimony as properly relates to it.

In quoting from the text of Isaiah, we shall adopt
the translation of Delitzsch, one of the most learned
and evangelical Jews of our own day, partly because
it is his nation whom the book he translates con-
demns, and partly because of the critical fulness and
fidelity of his translation. We would also acknowledge our indebtedness to the same expositor, for
many valuable suggestions in connection with the
text.

Jehovah Himself is Israel's accuser. It is God,
and not man, who renders the verdict against her,
and pronounces the sentence of her judicial condemnation: " Hear, O heavens," cries the prophet, "and
give ear, O earth ; for Jehovah speaketh."

"I have brought up children, and raised them high, and
they have fallen away from me. An ox knoweth its owner,
and an ass its master's crib : Israel doth not know, my
people doth not consider."

That is ; the nation which stands so peculiarly in
the relation of children to Me, and to whom I stand
so peculiarly in the relation of their heavenly Father ;

My children, whom I have begotten by my promise to their father Abraham, that I would make of him a great nation, and bless them that blessed them, and curse them that cursed them ; and by so many manifestations of My almighty power and sovereign grace in their behalf; *Israel*, so called after Jacob, their father, who wrestled with Me for a blessing upon himself and his descendants, and prevailed with Me ; " *My people*," the nation which I have chosen out of all other nations to be the nation of My possession, and My Own peculiar government ;—they have rebelled against Me; they have fallen away from Me ; their rebellion and apostasy have been persisted in so long, and have reached such a height, that it has become, at last, simply inhuman : they have sunk to a lower level than the brutes : they have not even their instinctive knowledge and perception. " An ox knoweth its owner, and an ass its master's crib : Israel doth not know, my people doth not consider."

Such is Jehovah's accusation against Israel. Such is Jehovah's piercing and hopeless lamentation over the apostate nation. The divine grief is even a more affecting accusation against the ungodly nation, than the divine condemnation itself.

Here the words of Jehovah end. The prophet now breaks forth with uncontrollable vexation against the ungrateful and ungodly nation.

" Woe upon the sinful nation, the guilt-laden people, the miscreant race, the children acting corruptly! They have forsaken Jehovah, blasphemed Israel's Holy One, turned away backwards."

That is; according to the choice and determination of God, Israel was to be a holy nation, but by her own sinful choice and guilty self-determination, by the weight and magnitude of her sins, and her confirmed apostasy of thought and word and deed—as if, indeed, she were the seed, not of the covenanted patriarchs, but of evil-doers only—she has now become the meet subject, not only of Jehovah's hopeless

lamentation over her, but of lamentation filled with
judicial wrath. "Woe upon the sinful nation!"

"Why would ye be perpetually smitten, multiplying
rebellion? Every head is diseased, and every heart is sick?"

That is; why are ye so foolish as to heap apostasy
upon apostasy, and continue to call down upon yourselves the judgments of God, which have already
fallen upon you, blow after blow? Your apostasy has
reached such a pass, that in all the nation there is
not one head or heart, that is not morally and totally
diseased with sin. Surely you have been sufficiently
smitten by the wrath of God to have been brought
to reflection. But, alas! the whole nation is one
miserably diseased body.

"From the soul of the foot even to the head there is
nothing sound in it; cuts, and stripes, and festering wounds;
they have not been pressed out, nor bound up, nor has there
been any soothing with oil."

That is; the nation has rejected the merciful and
compassionate kindness of God so long; and the
cure which He has so continually offered to effect,
and has now at last become so miserably and totally
diseased throughout, that there is no health in it, or
any hope of it. In a word, it is all over with the
guilty nation. The day of forgiveness is past.

The body, thus inwardly and outwardly diseased,
evidently includes both the people and the land, in
their alike fearful condition in the prophet's time; for
he thus with sharp and broken sentences proceeds:

"Your land . . . . a desert; your cities . . . . burned
with fire; your field . . . . foreigners consuming it before your eyes, and a desert like overthrowing by strangers."

What a literal fulfilment and perfect realization of
the curses of the law, as recorded in Lev. xxvi and
Deut. xxviii and xxix, the latter of which we have
cited; and that not only in the time of Isaiah, but
ever since!

"And the daughter of Zion remains like a hut in a vineyard; like a hammock in a cucumber field, as a besieged city."

That is; although thus surrounded by the desolations of the land, Jerusalem has, through the omnipotent mercy of God, escaped the curses of the law; even as the prophet goes on to say :

"Unless Jehovah of hosts had left us a little of what had escaped, we had become like Sodom, we were like Gomorrah."

The prophet, having thus affirmed that nothing but the mercy of God had saved Israel from utter desolation and destruction, and spared, as yet, Jerusalem, now changes the current of his address, as if anticipating that the nation would justify itself against these accusations, by an appeal to its scrupulous observance of the law; and thus launches forth the accusations of Jehovah anew:

"Hear the word of Jehovah, ye Sodom judges; give ear to the law of our God, O, Gomorrah nation! What is the multitude of your slain-offerings to me ? saith Jehovah. I am satiated with the whole offerings of rams, and the fat of stalled calves; and blood of bullocks and sheep and he-goats I do not like."

That is; to what purpose the multitude of your sacrifices, when offered unto Me with such hollow formality, such hypocritical and ceremonial righteousness only ? I am weary of them. I want no more of them. I never desired them. The prophet continues in the same strain :

"When ye come to appear before my face, who hath required this at your hand, to tread my courts ? Continue not to bring lying meat-offerings; abomination incense is it to me. New-moon and Sabbath, calling of festal meetings; I cannot bear ungodliness and a festal crowd. Your new-moons and your festive seasons my soul hateth ; they have become a burden to me; I am weary of bearing them. And if ye stretch out your hands, I hide my eyes from you ; if ye make ever so much praying I do not hear, your hands are full of blood."

Thus the last bulwark of their self-righteousness was now swept away. Even their praying, an instinct common to all men who recognize a Supreme Being, however ignorantly, had become an abomination to God.

As we have already asked, what crowning sin could the nation now commit, that would render it more deserving of God's judicial wrath?

We come now to the judicial sentence itself.

Isaiah is admitted into the personal presence of the "Holy One of Israel," by Whom is meant in the scene of the present vision, as St. John, the evangelist, informs us (John xii, 41), the Second Person of the Godhead, or Christ Himself. This appellation, in the twenty-nine instances of its use by Isaiah—but five times is it elsewhere used in the Old-Testament Scriptures, three times in the Psalms, and twice in Jeremiah—uniformly refers to the Messiah alone.

"I saw," says the prophet, "the Lord of all sitting upon a high and exalted throne, and his borders filling the temple."

That is; the prophet, being carried up into heaven, beheld, seated upon a high and exalted throne, which was the heavenly antitype of the earthly throne formed by the ark of the covenant in the earthly temple, the Lord of all in human form, His robes filling the temple.

"Above it stood seraphim : each one had six wings; with two he covered his face, and with two he covered his feet, and with two he did fly. And one cried to the other, and said, Holy, holy, holy is Jehovah of hosts: filling the whole earth is His glory."

The seraphim here described are nowhere else mentioned in the Holy Scriptures, and are supposed to be the media or messengers of the fire of the divine love, as the cherubim are supposed to be the media or messengers of the fire of the divine wrath. Their ascription of holiness to the Lord is undoubtedly to be understood in the same sense with the doxology of the four living creatures described in the Revelation (Rev. iv, 8); " Holy, holy, holy, Lord God Almighty, Who was, and is, and is to come." This ascription of the seraphim does not mean, that when Isaiah thus beheld them, the whole earth, or any part of it, and least of all the nation of Israel, was filled with the glory of Jehovah; but that, when the purposes of God in behalf of Israel, and, through Israel, in behalf of all mankind, should all be accomplished, towards the fulfilment of which the judicial blinding of Israel had now become a necessary step, then the whole earth should be filled with His glory, even as Jehovah sware unto Moses in the wilderness, "As truly as I live, all the earth shall be filled with the glory of the Lord." It is the ultimate and complete triumph only, the millennial triumph, of the merciful purposes of Jehovah, that is contemplated by both of these sublime doxologies; a result, however, which could only be accomplished, in consistency with the principles of God's holy government, by the employment, not less of the divine justice, than of the divine mercy, as God in His holy providence has always shown.

This judicial and retributive blinding of Israel, if we short-sighted mortals could but see it in its true light, was as necessary to her final salvation, as well as to the vindication of the divine glory, as was her Egyptian captivity before, or her Babylonian captivity afterwards, or her Roman, or more general Gentile captivity now. What may seem to us at the time but unfeeling vengeance in the necessary execution of justice upon a hardened and incorrigible criminal, may prove, in the end, the greatest mercy that could be displayed towards him. Was it not a mercy to Israel thus to arrest her in mid-career, and blind her eyes to the terrible enormity of her guilt?

It is not material to inquire whether this threefold ascription of the seraphim of holiness to the Lord is used in any intended symbolic sense or reference, as the symbol of the expanded unity of the Godhead,

three being the number, which, with the key-note,
produces a perfect chord. The antiphonal chorus of
the seraphim is here of interest to us alone, as showing
the holiness and purity of the presence into which
the prophet was thus graciously admitted; in which
divine and seraphic presence he was about to receive
the absolution of his sins, preparatory to his commission to pronounce the sentence of judicial blindness upon his own guilty but beloved Israel.

The prophet, at first entranced and overwhelmed
by the ineffable splendor of the scene, recovering his
self-possession, exclaims :—

"Woe is me! for I am lost; for I am a man of unclean
lips, and I am dwelling among a people of unclean lips;
for mine eyes have seen the King, Jehovah of hosts. And
one of the seraphim flew to me with a red-hot coal in his
hand. which he had taken with the tongs from the altar.
And he touched my mouth with it, and said, Behold this
hath touched thy lips, and thine iniquity is taken away;
and so thy sin is expiated. Then I heard the voice of the
Lord, saying. whom shall I send. and who will go for us.
Then I said, Behold me here; send me."

We recognize in connection with this whole scene, its
heavenly splendor, the divine and seraphic presence,
the sublime doxology of the seraphim, the office
which they filled in connection with the divine
holiness and love, and the seraphic absolution of the
prophet's sins, not only the lofty and peculiar fitness
of Isaiah to become the ministerial agent of so terrible a sentence, but his no less lofty and peculiar
identification with the divine purposes in respect to
the ultimate triumph and glory of Christ's millennial
kingdom, and his equal fitness to be, at the same
time, above all others, alike the great judicial and
great millennial prophet of Israel, as we have already
described him.

Listen now to the commission in which the heavenly
scene reaches its awful consummation :—

"*He said, Go, and tell this people* [not My
people, *this* people], *Hear on, and understand*

not; and look on, but perceive not [These gerun-
dives imply the prolonged continuance of the
sentence]. *Make ye the heart of this people greasy,
and their ears heavy, and their eyes sticky* [These
imperatives are not to be understood as simply a
commission to the prophet to tell the people what
God had determined to do. They imply, in an in-
tensive sense, the idea and continuous process of
hardening, with God as the principal and efficient
cause, the message the mediate cause, and the
prophet the ministerial cause]; *that they may not
see with their eyes, and hear with their ears, and
their heart understand, and they be converted, and
one heal them.*"

How mournful the commission! How terrible the
sentence! How terribly opposite to the seraphic
mission the prophet had experienced in himself!
The seraph had absolved Isaiah with the burning coal,
not that he as a prophet might absolve, but harden
his people by his word; that he might be the prophet
of the destruction, not less than of the ultimate
salvation of his nation.

Such was the sentence of judicial blindness that
ever afterwards hung over Israel during the re-
mainder of the Old-Testament dispensation; which
hung over her during the whole earthly ministry of
her Messiah; to which He so often and with such infinite sorrow alluded; which He declared to be the
reason why He spake to the multitudes in parables,
explaining them not, and not in more intelligible
forms of speech; with which He would never interfere, but only reaffirm, and ever reaffirm, though the
heavens and the earth should pass away. Indeed it
was the Messiah of Israel Himself Who was the Author
of the sentence, and appointed, as we shall directly
see, the term of its continuance; and will He reverse
His Own decree, before its appointed term expires?
" Think not I am come to destroy the law or the
prophets: I am not come to destroy, but to fulfil.
For verily I say unto you, Till heaven and earth

pass, one jot or one tittle shall in no wise pass from
the law, till all be fulfilled." Such, finally, is the
sentence which hangs over Israel now, and will continue to hang over her, " till all shall be fulfilled."
Nothing, since this sentence of judicial blindness was
first pronounced, has ever availed to reach the insensible heart of the guilty nation, and nothing
ever will, " till all shall be fulfilled." Israel's Messiah, in His personal ministry upon the earth, as com-
pletely abandoned the nation to its judicial blindness, as He so abandoned it in the vision in which He
appeared to Isaiah ; and His apostles followed His
example : and abandoned thereto will it remain,
until His feet shall stand again upon the Mount of
Olives, and Israel shall reach the fearful climax of
her supernatural servitude and affliction under her
present judicial dispensation, all human schemes and
speculations to the contrary notwithstanding.

Henceforward, Israel's judicial blindness, her judicial insensibility of heart, her hopelessly incorrigible
impenitence and unbelief, is an element which enters
into the preaching of Isaiah, and of all the succeeding
prophets, and no less into the teachings of Christ and
His apostles. Henceforward, a moral night of deep-
est darkness and impenetrable gloom, in fulfilment
of this sentence, settles down upon the judicially-
blinded nation. The prophets and the apostles and
Christ Himself invariably recognize Israel's total
want of moral understanding and perception even,
and the utter hopelessness of preaching repentance
to the nation, or seeking to reclaim it from its sins,
" till all shall be fulfilled," at the close of her judicial
dispensation, against the apostate and abandoned
nation. Especially was the fearful condemnation
which rested upon the nation, ever present to the
mind of the prophet who first pronounced it. At a
later period of his ministry, he refers to it in the
strongest terms (chap. xliv, 18). So also Jeremiah
(v, 21). So also Ezekiel (xii, 2).

So also, under the New-Testament dispensation,

does the apostle Paul refer to it as an irrevocable decree, which had gone forth against the nation, and was to last until the close of her present judicial dispensation; or, to use his own words, "till the fulness of the Gentiles be come in;" or, to use the words of our Saviour, expressive of precisely the same meaning, "until the times of the Gentiles shall be fulfilled." Says Paul, "Israel hath not obtained that which she seeketh for; but the election hath obtained it, and the rest [the nation at large] were blinded; according as it is written [Is. xxix, 9–12], God hath given them the spirit of slumber, eyes that they should not see, and ears that they should not hear, unto this day. And David saith [Ps. lxix, 22, 23], Let their table be made a snare, and a trap, and a stumbling-block, and a recompense unto them: Let their eyes be darkened, that they may not see, and bow down their back always."

So again, the same apostle, having expounded the Scriptures "out of the law of Moses, and out of the prophets, from morning till evening," to certain Jews who came to him at Rome, vexed at last by their total moral insensibility, and total want of moral perception, thus dismissed them from his presence; "Well spake the Holy Ghost by Esaias the prophet unto our fathers, saying, Go unto this people, and say, Hearing ye shall hear, and not understand; and seeing ye shall see, and not perceive; for the heart of this people is waxed gross, and their ears are dull of hearing, and their eyes have they closed; lest they should see with their eyes, and hear with their ears, and understand with their heart, and should be converted and I should heal them. Be it known therefore unto you, that the salvation of God is sent unto the Gentiles, and they will hear it." Acts xxviii, 23–29.

Did the apostle Paul give way to discouragement and despondency, when he thus encountered an obstacle so insurmountable to his preaching, as the judicial blindness of his nation? Not at all. It is immediately added, that "Paul dwelt two whole years

[at Rome] in his own hired house, and received all
that came in unto him, preaching the kingdom of
God, and teaching those things which concern the
Lord Jesus Christ *with all confidence*, no man for-
bidding him."

Paul cheated not himself with any of the rose-colored
and delusive expectations, with which it is so often and
so unscripturally sought to stimulate the tardy piety
of our own times. He was content if none, who were
appointed unto salvation, failed of the grace of God
by any want of diligence on his part; " For I speak
to you, Gentiles, inasmuch as I am the apostle of the
Gentiles, I magnify my office; if by any means I may
provoke to emulation those which are my flesh, and
may save some of them." " *Save some of them!*"
This was the mark towards which this wonderful
apostle pressed forward for the prize of his high
calling.

Again; St. John, the Evangelist, briefly summing
up, after the supper at Bethany, the results of the
ministry of our Saviour, and alluding to its unsuccessful termination, so far as the nation at large was
concerned, says :—

"But though He had done so many mighty works before
them, yet they believed not on him: that the saying of Esaias
the prophet might be fulfilled, which he spake, Lord who
hath believed our report? and to whom hath the arm of the
Lord been revealed? Therefore they could not believe, because that Esaias said again, He hath blinded their eyes,
and hardened their hearts; that they should not see with
their eyes, nor understand with their heart, and be converted,
and I should heal them." John xii. 37–40.

The immediately following words of the Evangelist show that it was the Second Person of the Godhead, the Messiah of Israel Himself, Who appeared
to Isaiah in the vision.

" *These things said Esaias, when he saw his
glory, and spake of him.*" v. 41.

How manifestly, also, did our Saviour recognize
the impassible barrier which the judicial blindness

of the nation presented to His Own ministry. Weeping over Jerusalem just at the close of His earthly ministry, how sorrowfully He exclaimed! " O, that thou, even thou, at least in this thy day, hadst known the things that belong to thy peace; but now they are hid from thine eyes!"

So, also, at an earlier period of His ministry, did He expressly assure His disciples that the judicial blindness of the nation was the reason why He spake to it in parables.

"Therefore speak I to them in parables; because they seeing see not; and hearing they hear not; neither do they understand. And in them is *refulfilled* the prophecy of Esaias. By hearing ye shall hear. and shall not understand; and seeing ye shall see, and shall not perceive; for this people's heart is waxed gross, and their ears are dull of hearing, and their eyes have they closed; lest at any time they should see with their eyes, and hear with their ears, and should understand with their hearts, and should be converted, and I should heal them." Matt. xiii, 13-15.

The depth and totality of their judicial blindness is made still more manifest and impressive by the contrast presented to the nation at large by His concluding words to His disciples:—

" But blessed are your eyes, for they see; and your ears, for they hear." v. 16.

That is; *you*, my disciples, and the faithful remnant, the election of grace, of which you are, and which you represent, are able to understand and believe the secrets of my spiritual kingdom; the riches of my free salvation; the mysteries of my redeeming love; the infinite atonement of my precious blood; my redemptive title to the usurped sovereignty of lost and fallen Israel, and of a lost and ruined world. But *they* do not, and cannot, understand. They know not, neither do they consider. They have sunk to a lower level than the brutes, and have not even their instinctive knowledge and perception. They are dead in their trespasses and sins and unbelief. They are wholly destitute of spiritual

discernment. They are insensible alike to the ap-
peals of mercy, and to the chastisements of wrath.
They despise, and reject, and deride, and persecute
Me. They obstinately deny My rightful claims, both
as their temporal Messiah, as their own records
show, and as their spiritual Messiah, as is attested
by My mighty works. They blaspheme Me, charging
Me that I cast out devils by Beelzebub the prince of
the devils. They grieve away the Holy Spirit in this
His Own peculiar dispensation. They reproach Me
for My obscure origin and humble followers, My
fastings and My tears, and make Me the song even
of the drunkards in their gates.

And yet how the forgiving heart of our Saviour
melts over the sinful nation! "O! Jerusalem, Jerusalem, thou that killest the prophets, and stonest
them which are sent unto thee; how often would I
have gathered thy children together even as a hen
gathereth her chickens under her wings, and *ye
would not.*" Matt. xxiii, 37.   Therefore—

"Because I have called, and ye have refused; I
have stretched out my hand, and no man regarded;
but ye have set at naught all my counsels, and would
none of my reproof; I also will laugh at your ca-
lamity; I will mock when your fear cometh; when
your fear cometh as desolation; and your destruction
cometh as a whirlwind; when distress and anguish
cometh upon you. Then shall they call upon me, but
I will not answer; they shall seek me early, but they
shall not find me; for that they hated knowledge,
and did not choose the fear of the Lord; they would
none of my counsel; they despised all my reproof.
Therefore shall they eat of the fruit of their own
way, and be filled with their own devices. For the
ease of the simple shall slay them, and the prosperity of fools shall destroy them." Prov. i, 24–32.
And yet, alas! "How shall I give thee up, Ephraim?
how shall I deliver thee, Israel? how shall I make thee
as Admah? how shall I set thee as Zeboim? mine
heart is turned within me, my repentings are kin-

ISRAEL'S JUDICIAL BLINDNESS.

died together. I will not execute the fierceness of mine anger. I will not return to destroy Ephraim; for I am God, and not man; the Holy One in the midst of thee." Hosea xi, 8–9. 'Fain would I draw them even now,' does our Saviour seem to say, as for the last time He wept over untoward Israel, " with the cords of a man, with the bonds of love, and take off the yoke on their jaws, and lay meat unto them;" but now, alas! it is only left to Me to foretell to them the certain judicial consequences of their own sinful conduct as judicially-condemned criminals, which, when they are all fulfilled upon them, and they are moved upon by the Spirit of grace, and of supplications which I will pour upon them at My second coming, at the expiration of their judicial sentence and dispensation, may prove the means of bringing them, at last, to repentance; for, as I told them in the wilderness, I am a merciful and long-suffering God, forgiving iniquity, transgression and sin. Therefore I speak to them in parables, that their own past, present and future sinful conduct, thus ever held up in a prophetic mirror before them, may, at last, in their own sight condemn them. It is the only hope. Thus only, while justice is satisfied, can mercy supervene, and triumph in the end. " For I would not, brethren, that ye should be ignorant of this mystery, lest ye should be wise in your own conceits, that blindness in part is happened to Israel, until the fulness of the Gentiles be come in. And so all Israel shall be saved: as it is written, There shall come out of Zion the Deliverer, and shall turn away ungodliness from Jacob; *for this is my covenant unto them, when I shall take away their sins.*" Rom. xi, 25–27.

Thus perished guilty Israel in her sins. Thus was she condemned to eat of the fruit of her own ways, and to be filled with her own devices. All was in vain to save her. The warnings of the prophets, whom, one after another, she smote, and killed, and stoned, are at last all justified ; and now the wicked

husbandmen seek the life of the son and heir. Moses;
Isaiah; Christ; the burning bush, with its unconsum-
ing flames; the burning altar, with its seraphic
choirs; the star of Bethlehem, with its angel choirs;
the baptism of water, the baptism of the Holy Ghost,
and the baptism of fire; the persuasions of the divine
love, the beating and trembling waves of the divine
wrath; all, all was in vain. The prophet who pronounced the sentence of judicial blindness was sawn
in sunder. Its divine Author and Ratifier was put to
the ignominious death, *servile supplicium*, of a
Roman slave, bearing His Own cross to the sacrifice.
Well might the conscious and astonished earth shake
with horror, and veil itself in darkness at the scene!

But a holy remnant remains: it always has re-
mained: it always will remain: it always has been
preserved: it always will be preserved: a holy seed:
" to whom [effectually] pertaineth the adoption, and
the glory, and the covenants, and the giving of the
law, and the service of God, and the promises," and
through whom all Israel will finally be saved. Well
did Isaiah exclaim, " Except the Lord of Sabaoth
had left us a seed, we had been as Sodom, and had
been made like unto Gomorrah."

" And is there still a tenth therein, this also is
given up to destruction, like the terebinth and like
the oak, of which, when they are felled, only a root-
stump remains: such a root-stump is a holy seed."

Cut down the aged oak or terebinth of Palestine
to the very roots. Out of the battered stump a new
shoot will spring, a holy nation, a royal priesthood,
a chosen generation, a rod out of the worn-out stem
of Jesse, a fruitful branch out of the withered root
of David; and the wilderness and the solitary place
shall be glad for them, and the desert shall rejoice
and blossom as the rose; it shall blossom abundantly,
even with joy and singing. Then " the eyes of them
that see, shall not be dim; and the ears of them that
hear, shall hearken."

But when, the inquiry now arises, will the sentence

of Israel's judicial blindness, the term of her judicial condemnation, expire?

The divine Author of the sentence has told us, in answer to the same inquiry made of Him by Isaiah. He replied; " until towns are wasted without inhabitant, and the houses without man, and the ground shall be laid waste, a wilderness, and Jehovah shall put men far away, and there shall be many forsaken places within the land." Isa. vi, 11.

This reply, however definite as to the desolating consequences, is not definite as to any prophetic and related point of time, or prophetic and related order of events, in concurrence with which the sentence will be finally fulfilled.

But the Divine Author of the sentence, in answer to essentially the same inquiry, made of Him by His disciples, just before the close of His personal ministry, renders both the prophetic and related point of time and the prophetic and related order of events in connection with which the term of Israel's judicial blindness will expire, perfectly clear and definite. " They (Israel) shall fall by the edge of the sword, and shall be led away captive into all nations: and Jerusalem shall be trodden down of the Gentiles, until the times of the Gentiles be fulfilled. * * * Then look up, and lift up your heads; for your redemption draweth nigh." Luke xxi, 24-33.

The term of Israel's judicial blindness will therefore cease, when "the times of the Gentiles shall be fulfilled," and when, in connection therewith, all the prophetic judgments, both of the Old and the New-Testament, revelations, including the judicial prophecies of the parables, shall be finally accomplished upon her.

But when, the supplementary inquiry arises, will the times of the Gentiles be fulfilled, since then it is that the term of Israel's judicial blindness will cease? This inquiry appears to us to be susceptible, upon the testimony of the prophetic Scriptures, of a perfectly clear and definite answer; not however, in respect to any precise, independent, and absolute, or, indeed, proximate date, chronologically determined, or determinable; but in respect only and clearly, to the precise and related order of certain future events; which events are frequently spoken of in the prophetic Scriptures as occurring simultaneously, at the close of the present dispensation, or order of things. These events are rarely, if ever, described or referred to in prophetic Scripture as isolated events. They are never confounded with any other events. It is impossible to mistake them, or the related time and order of their occurrence, at the close of the present dispensation, or rather, which more especially concerns our present theme, at the conjunction, before referred to, of Israel's judicial and millennial dispensations. They form a wholly distinct group by themselves. They are clearly stated and defined, and often in their inseparable relation to one another. There is not a constellation in our nightly heavens, that presents to the eye a clearer outline, or shines with a more distinct and constant lustre, than this particular group of events upon the prophetic pages. Three of them only, however, although there are others of not less vital consequence, enter into our present inquiry, as to when the times of the Gentiles will be fulfilled, namely :—

1. The second advent of the Messiah of Israel.

2. The simultaneous deliverance of Israel from her Gentile oppressors, and the introduction of her millennial dispensation.

3. The complete and final overthrow of Gentile ascendency over Israel, and the close of the probationary dispensation of the Gentile nations.

To obtain a correct view of the three events to which we here refer, in their mutually related occurrence, we must first briefly advert to the prophetic history of the Jewish nation as it approaches the close of the present dispensation.

Israel will first be restored, and, as a nation, be reinstated in her own land, and exercise all the func-

tions of an organized nationality therein, as com-
pletely as ever before, or as ever any other nation.
Under the leadership of Antichrist, the last great
monarch of the Gentiles, the ungodly and confede-
rated Gentile nations—the victims of a greater than
Israel's judicial blindness, of the "strong delusion" to which the apostle Paul refers in his Second
Epistle to the Thessalonian Church (2 Thess. ii,
8–12), and jealous, we may well suppose, of the great
wealth and political power of Israel, of the fore-
shadowing of her coming ascendency and exaltation, and of her still professed allegiance to the God
of Israel—will gather themselves together, by their
representative hosts, against Jerusalem, there to
enact the closing scene of that great tribulation, to which, under Antichrist, she will have been
subjected, "a tribulation such as never was since
there was a nation, no, nor ever shall be."* It is at
this point that prophecy takes up the description of
the final conflict between Israel and the nations of
the Gentiles, the time of the occurrence of which is
so often denominated in the prophetic Scriptures,
"the day of the Lord," or "day of visitation," when
the Spirit of the Lord shall set up a standard against
the enemies of Israel, and the Redeemer shall come
again to Zion.

Before proceeding, however, to the prophetic evidence of the joint occurrence of the three events to
which we have referred; namely, the second advent
of the Messiah of Israel, the deliverance of Israel,
and the final overthrow of Gentile ascendency in the
earth, we must not omit to call attention to a conclusion from our foregoing reasoning, of the highest
prophetic consequence.

We have never seen it claimed by any sacred wri-
ter or expositor, that a millennium is to be enjoyed
upon the earth, under the present Gospel dispensation,
which shall not include the nation of Israel. In-

---

* For a statement of the proofs on these points, see "The Anti-
Christ of Prophecy," in "Briefs on Prophetic Themes."

deed, it is universally admitted, that one of the most
prominent and glorious features of the expected
millennium will be the full realization of God's ancient covenants concerning Israel and Jerusalem.

Now if Israel and Jerusalem are to be trodden
down of the Gentiles, or, which is the same thing,
are to remain under their present judicial condemnation, until the times of the Gentiles shall be fulfilled,
and if the times of the Gentiles are not to be fulfilled
until the close of the present Gentile dispensation,
how is it possible that God's covenants of blessing
with Israel and Jerusalem should be fulfilled, so
long as the times of the Gentiles remain unfulfilled,
so long as the present dispensation is still uncon-
cluded, and the treading-down of Israel, and her
judicial blindness are still unaccomplished upon
her?

But God's ancient covenants will at some time be
fulfilled.   His promises are forever sure.   He is a
covenant-keeping God.   And if His covenants with
His covenant-people have not been fulfilled in a past
dispensation, or in the past of the present dispensation, and are not to be fulfilled in the future of the
present dispensation, when, we ask, will they be fulfilled, if not in a future dispensation? and must not
such future dispensation, because of their fulfilment,
be a millennial dispensation? must it not be *the* millennial dispensation? or, if there is to be any other
millennium, or a millennium at any other time, when,
what, and where, and by what authority?   Is there
to be a millennium, in which Israel, as a nation, and
the covenants and promises of God concerning Israel
are not to be included? a Gentile millennium with
Israel left out?   God forbid!

What is thus true of the ancient Jewish covenants
is equally true of the millennial visions of Isaiah,
which are wholly based upon them, and can only be
fulfilled when they are fulfilled; which can pertain
only to the dispensation to which they pertain, and
not to Israel under her present judicial condemna-

tion, under the curse of judicial blindness which, at present, rests upon her. The same is also true of the millennial predictions of the Psalms, and of all millennial predictions whatever.

We now invite the attention of our readers to a few

SCRIPTURAL TESTIMONIES,

with brief comments thereon, relating to the termination of the sentence of Israel's judicial blindness ; to the post-judicial and pre-millennial advent of the Messiah of Israel for the deliverance of His people and the destruction of their foes ; and to some of the incidents and scenes concurrent therewith, and consequent thereupon, as the millennial years roll on. These testimonies, left to their own simple utterance and self-interpreting and unaided light, will be found, as we believe, to establish, with Scriptural certainty, in perfect harmony with all prophetic analogy, and without affording the least support or encouragement to any vague and contravening spiritualistic hypothesis, the following plain inferences of fact and literal and incontrovertible conclusions. It should, however, be remembered, first and always, in considering these conclusions, that all prophecy, descending from the same heavenly source, seeks the untroubled waters of the same immeasurable sea; that prophecy, viewing it from its highest Scriptural point of view, is to be regarded as a broad and mighty stream, pressing ever forward with spreading banks and swelling volume, till lost in the great deep of God's fulfilled purposes concerning Israel and Jerusalem ; the one great supreme event and crowning glory of that blessed consummation ever being the personal return to the earth of the Holy One of Israel, not, however, as the jealous Deliverer and recognized Messiah of His Own people only, but as the victorious and everlasting sovereign of a recovered earth, the blessed and only Mediator and Redeemer of lost mankind; Israel being the chosen instrument and example, through which alone, in the merciful counsels of Omnipotence, the millennial and heavenly goals will at last be won by the spared inhabitants of the earth.

In presenting these testimonies to our readers, we shall cite, in the first place, certain prophecies which look forward to the consummation of the present dispensation; and, in the second place, certain other prophecies which are descriptive of its actual incidents and scenes, as well as of some of the earthly and millennial scenes which lie beyond.

The facts and conclusions referred to are as follows:—

1. The joint occurrence of the three events to which we have referred; namely, the personal return of the Messiah of Israel to the earth; the simultaneous deliverance of Israel from Gentile oppression; and the fulfilment of the times of the Gentiles, or everlasting overthrow of Gentile supremacy in the earth.

2. The continuance of Israel in her present downtrodden condition—that is, under her present judicial condemnation, or sentence of judicial blindness—until the consummation of these three events.

3. The total absence of any allusion in these prophecies to a general and final judgment of mankind, as occurring in connection with these events; and of any allusion to the heavenly or eternal state as immediately supervening thereupon.

4. The fact that they contain, on the other hand, a full and minute description of an earthly condition or order of things, thereafterwards ensuing, in respect both to the moral and spiritual, the domestic, social and national interests, concerns and affairs of the Jewish nation, and of mankind at large; which can belong only to another and purely earthly dispensation or economy; which belongs not to the heavenly or eternal state, and must therefore precede it: a con-

dition or order of things, which answers fully, and precisely, and at all points, to the terms of God's ancient covenants and promises concerning Israel and Jerusalem, and to the millennial visions of Isaiah and other prophets; and which cannot co-exist with Israel's unfulfilled sentence of judicial blindness.

The prophetic testimony upon these points we now present to our readers; citing, as said before, in the first place, certain prophecies which look forward, in more general terms, to the close of the present dispensation; and, in the second place, other prophecies which are descriptive of its actual incidents and scenes.

Moses:—

"And it shall come to pass, when all these things are come upon thee, the blessing and the curse, which I have set before thee, and thou shalt call them to mind among all the nations, whither the Lord thy God hath driven thee, and shalt return unto the Lord thy God, and shalt obey his voice according to all that I command thee this day, thou and thy children, with all thy heart, and with all thy soul; that then the Lord thy God will turn thy captivity, and have compassion upon thee, and will return and gather thee from all the nations, whither the Lord thy God hath scattered thee. And the Lord thy God will bring thee into the land which thy fathers possessed, and thou shalt possess it; and he will do thee good and multiply thee above thy fathers And the Lord thy God will circumcise thine heart, and the heart of thy seed, to love the Lord thy God with all thine heart, and with all thy soul, that thou mayest live. And the Lord thy God will put all these curses upon thine enemies, and on them that hate thee, which persecuted thee. And thou shalt return and obey the voice of the Lord, and do all his commandments, which I command thee this day. And the Lord thy God will make thee plenteous in every work of thine hand, in the fruit of thy body and in the fruit of thy cattle, and in the fruit of thy land, for good; for the Lord will again rejoice over thee for good, as he rejoiced over thy fathers." Deut. xxx, 1-10.

The period here referred to is most clearly, by the terms of the prediction, subsequent to the present dispersion of Israel among the Gentiles, and must, therefore, be still future.

"And it shall come to pass, if thou shalt hearken diligently unto the voice of the Lord thy God, to observe and do all the commandments which I command thee this day, that the Lord thy God will set thee on high above all nations of the earth." Deut. xxviii, 1.

"If they shall confess their iniquity, and the iniquity of their fathers, with their trespasses which they trespassed against me, and also that they have walked contrary unto me, and that I also have walked contrary unto them, and have brought them into the land of their enemies; if then their uncircumcised hearts be humbled, and they then accept of the punishment of their iniquity; then will I remember my covenant with Jacob, and also my covenant with Isaac, and also my covenant with Abraham will I remember, and I will remember the land." Levit. xxvi, 40–42.

God has never yet fulfilled these covenants with Abraham and Isaac and Jacob, in any full and just sense. These covenants are everlasting covenants; everlasting, when once fulfilled, in their continuance and their enjoyment, and wholly preclude the idea of subsequent apostasy or falling away; and Israel is now suffering utter desolation, both as a nation and as a land, in consequence of her disobedience and apostasies, in fulfilment of the sentence of her judicial blindness, and will continue to suffer utter desolation "until all shall be fulfilled," and she shall say, "Blessed is he that cometh in the name of the Lord."

That the covenants of blessing to Israel, one and all, when once actually realized and fulfilled, will be realized and fulfilled for all coming time, and will never suffer any abeyance or abatement in their full and glorious fruition to the end of time, is as clearly revealed as that they will not, and cannot be realized and fulfilled, or begin to be realized and fulfilled, until the no less irrevocable covenant of Israel's judicial blindness shall expire, at the close of her present judicial dispensation. The prophetic evidence to this effect is simply overwhelming. Our limits will admit only of the briefest reference to it.

"And I will bring again the captivity of my people of

Israel, and they shall build the waste cities, and inhabit them, and they shall plant vineyards, and drink the wine thereof; they shall also make gardens, and eat the fruit of them. And I will plant them upon their land, and they shall *no more be pulled out of their land* which I have given them, saith the Lord thy God." Amos ix, 14, 15.

When, ever since this prophecy was uttered, have not the children of Israel, with rare intervals of possession, been pulled out of their land? When were they ever more pulled out of it, more scattered up and down the whole face of the earth, than they are now? When will they cease to be pulled out of it, so long as their sentence of judicial blindness remains unfulfilled?

" And I will make a covenant of peace, and will cause the evil beasts to cease out of the land; and they shall dwell safely in the wilderness, and sleep in the woods. And I will make them and the places round about my hill a blessing; and I will cause the shower to come down in his season; there shall be showers of blessing. And the tree of the field shall yield her fruit, and the earth shall yield her increase, and they shall be safe in their land, and shall know that I am the Lord, when I have broken the bands of their yoke, and delivered them out of the hand of those that served themselves of them. And they shall *no more* be a prey to the heathen, neither shall the beast of the land devour them; but they shall dwell safely, and none shall make them afraid. And I will raise up for them a plant of renown, and they shall *no more* be consumed with hunger in the land, neither bear the shame of the heathen *any more.* Then shall they know that I the Lord their God am with them, and that they, even the house of Israel, are my people, saith the Lord God." Ezekiel xxxiv, 25–30.

"Yea, I will rejoice over them to do them good, and I will plant them in this land assuredly with my whole heart and with my whole soul. For thus saith the Lord; Like as I have brought all this great evil upon this people, so will I bring upon them all the good that I have promised them." Jer. xxxii, 41, 42.

" Thy people also shall all be righteous: they shall *inherit the land forever*, the branch of my planting, the work of my hands, that I may be glorified." Is. ix, 21.

" Behold ! a king shall reign in righteousness, and princes shall rule in judgment, and the work of righteousness shall be peace ; and the effect of righteousness, quietness and assurance *forever:* and my people shall dwell in a peaceable habitation, and in sure dwellings, and in quiet resting-places." Isaiah, xxxii., 1, 17, 18.

"Egypt shall be a desolation, and Edom shall be a desolate wilderness. *But Judah shall dwell forever, and Jerusalem from generation to generation.* Joel iii, 21.

"For the nation and kingdom that will not serve thee shall perish; yea, those nations shall be utterly wasted. The glory of Lebanon shall come unto thee, the fir tree, the pine tree, and the box together, to beautify the place of my sanctuary; and I will make the place of my feet glorious.

" The sons also of them that afflicted thee shall come bending unto thee; and all they that despised thee shall bow themselves down at the soles of thy feet; and they shall call thee The city of the Lord, the Zion of the Holy One of Israel. And the name of the city, *from that day,* shall be, *The Lord is there.*" Is. lx, 12–14. Ez. xlviii, 35.

" Whereas thou hast been forsaken and hated, so that no man went through thee, I will make thee an *eternal* excellency, a joy of *many generations.*

"Thou shalt also suck the milk of the Gentiles, and shalt suck the breast of kings; and thou shalt know that I the Lord am thy Saviour and thy Redeemer, the Mighty One of Jacob." Is. lx, 14–16.

"For Zion's sake will I not hold my peace, and for Jerusalem's sake I will not rest, until the righteousness thereof go forth as brightness, and the salvation thereof as a lamp that burneth. And the Gentiles shall see thy righteousness, and all kings thy glory, and thou shalt be called by a new name, which the mouth of the Lord shall name. Thou shalt also be a crown of glory in the hand of the Lord, and a royal diadem in the hand of thy God. Thou shalt *no more* be termed Forsaken; neither shalt thy land *any more* be termed Desolate: but thou shalt be called Hephzibah, and thy land Beulah, and thy land shall be married. For as a young man marrieth a virgin, so shall thy sons marry thee: and as the bridegroom rejoiceth over the bride, so shall thy God rejoice over thee. The Lord hath sworn by his right hand, and by the arm of his strength. Surely I will *no more* give thy corn to be meat for thine enemies; and the sons of the stranger shall not drink thy wine, for the which thou hast labored; but they that have gathered it shall eat it, and praise the Lord; and they that have brought it together shall drink it in the courts of thy holiness. And they shall call them, The holy people, The redeemed of the Lord; and thou shalt be called, Sought out, A city not forsaken." Is. lxii, 1-5, 8, 9, 12.

Is it not the barest contradiction of terms, the purest solecism, a simply impossible supposition, the possible realization of these prophecies so long as the curse of Israel's judicial blindness, that most desolating of all the covenants of the divine wrath, remains unfulfilled? and unfulfilled we have seen that it will remain throughout the whole term of the present Gentile, or Gospel, dispensation, or, which is the same thing, until the times of the Gentiles are fulfilled; which is but a description, in other terms, of the limitation of Israel's judicial dispensation.

ISAIAH:— (Seven hundred and fifty years after Moses.)

"The Lord will have mercy upon Jacob, and will yet choose Israel, and set them in their own land, and the strangers shall be joined with them, and they shall cleave to the house of Jacob. And the peoples [the Gentile nations] shall take them and bring them to their place; and the house of Israel shall possess them in the land of the Lord, for servants and handmaids; and they shall rule over their oppressors. And it shall come to pass in the day that the Lord shall give thee rest from thy sorrow, and thy fear, and from the hard bondage wherein thou wast made to serve, that thou shalt take up this parable against the King of Babylon, and say, How hath the oppressed ceased! the golden city ceased! Is. xiv, 1-4.

It is equally clear that the allusion contained in this prophecy, which was uttered between two hundred and three hundred years after the reigns of David and Solomon, is to a period still in the future, for when, since it was uttered, has Israel been carried back to her place by the Gentile nations? When have Israel and Jacob made them captives whose captives they were, and possessed them for servants and handmaids in their own land?

When have they had rest from their sorrow, and their fear, and the hard bondage wherein they have been made to serve? When has the oppressor ceased? Was it after they were restored from their Babylonian captivity by Cyrus? But a remnant only of the two tribes of Judah and Benjamin—according to Josephus, forty-three thousand five hundred in number —were restored by Cyrus, and, instead of ruling over him, they were ruled over by him, while the ten lost tribes had been carried away, two hundred years before, into a captivity, from which they have never to this day returned, and in which no satisfactory trace of them has ever yet been discovered. In a word, when has this prophecy of Isaiah been fulfilled in the past? or, which is the same thing, when have the covenants of God concerning the nation and land of Israel, as expressed in this prophecy, ever been fulfilled, and the curse of judicial blindness consequently removed?

JEREMIAH:—(One hundred and thirty years after Isaiah.)

"Thus saith the Lord, again there shall be heard in this place, which ye say shall be *desolate without man* [the very words of the sentence of judicial blindness], and without inhabitants, and without beast, the voice of joy, and the voice of gladness, the voice of the bridegroom, and the voice of the bride, the voice of them that shall say, Praise the Lord of hosts; for he is good; for his mercy endureth forever; and of them that shall bring the sacrifice of praise unto the house of the Lord; for I will cause to return the captivity of the land as at the first.

"Thus saith the Lord of hosts, again in this place, which is desolate without man and without beast, and in all the cities thereof, shall be an habitation of shepherds causing their flocks to lie down. In the cities of the mountain, in the cities of the vale, and in the cities of the south, and in the land of Benjamin, and in the places about Jerusalem, and in the cities of Judah, shall the flocks pass again under the hands of him that telleth them, saith the Lord." Jer. xxxiii, 10–14.

Is it Israel under the present dispensation, under

the curse of judicial blindness, or is it Israel under
another dispensation, when the curse of judicial
blindness shall be lifted and removed, and when the
covenants shall be fulfilled, that is described in the
above prediction?

"In those days, and at that time, will I cause the branch
of righteousness to grow up unto David; and he shall execute judgment and righteousness in the land. In those
days shall Judah be saved, and Jerusalem shall dwell safely,
and this is the name wherewith she shall be called, the Lord
our righteousness. . . . . If my covenant be not with the day
and night, and if I have not appointed the ordinances of
heaven and earth; then will I cast away the seed of Jacob,
and David my servant. so that I will not take any of his
seed to be rulers over the seed of Abraham, Isaac and
Jacob, for I will cause their captivity to return, and have
mercy on them." Jer. xxxiii, 15, 16, 25, 26.

Does not this prediction as plainly and literally
foretell the future temporal and personal reign of the
Messiah of Israel, in millennial glory, upon the
throne of his father David, as it describes the revo-
lutions of day and night, to the certain and daily
fulfilment of His covenants with which God here com-
pares the certain fulfilment of His covenant with
David, concerning the Messiah's personal assumption
of his vacant throne? and is not this prediction descriptive of a dispensation, or order of things, which
can only ensue after the sentence of Israel's judicial
blindness has been removed, and the times of the
Gentiles are fulfilled? Can Jerusalem ever dwell
safely while she is "trodden down of the Gentiles?"

"Behold, the days come, saith the Lord, that I will make
a new covenant with the house of Israel, and with the house
of Judah; not according to the covenant that I made with
their fathers in the day that I took them by the hand to bring
them out of the land of Egypt; which my covenant they
brake, although I was an husband unto them. saith the
Lord. But this shall be the covenant that I will make with
the house of Israel; After those days, saith the Lord, I will
put my law in their inward parts, and write it in their hearts.
and will be their God, and they shall be my people. And

they shall teach no more every man his neighbor, and every man his brother, saying, Know the Lord ; for they shall all know me, from the least of them unto the greatest of them: for I will forgive their iniquity, and I will remember their sin no more." Jer. xxxi, 31–35.

The full, manifested glory of the new and everlasting covenant of grace, described in the above prediction, refers plainly enough to *a continuing earthly era or dispensation, after the sentence of Israel's judicial blindness shall have ceased:* that is, after the times of the Gentiles shall be fulfilled. The same is no less true of the following description of the final realization and triumph of the all-embracing Abrahamic covenant, which refers so expressly to Israel's final cure.

"Behold, I will bring it [Israel] health and cure, and will reveal unto them the abundance of peace and truth, and I will cause the captivity of Israel and the captivity of Judah to return, and will build them as at the first. And it [Jerusalem] shall be to me a name of joy, a praise and an honor before all the nations of the earth, which shall hear all the good that I do unto them; and they shall fear and tremble for all the goodness and all the prosperity that I procure unto it." Jer. xxxiii, 6–10.

We might multiply indefinitely predictions to the same effect from Isaiah down to the close of the Old Testament dispensation, all pointing to a period of time when Israel's judicial blindness shall end, and when, consequently, the times of the Gentiles shall be fulfilled.

We come now to the closing scenes of Israel's judicial dispensation, and the simultaneous judicial close of the probationary dispensation of the Gentile nations.

JOEL:—(Sixty years after Isaiah, and thirty-one after the extinction of the kingdom of Israel.)

"For, behold, in those days, and in that time, when I shall bring again the captivity of Judah and Jerusalem [never as yet]. I will also gather all nations, and will bring them down into the valley of Jehoshaphat, and will plead

with them there for my people and for my heritage Israel,
whom they have scattered among the nations and parted my
land. . . . . . Proclaim ye this among the Gentiles; Pre-
pare war, wake up the mighty men, let all the men of war
draw near; let them come up: beat your ploughshares into
swords, and your pruninghooks into spears: let the weak say
I am strong. Assemble yourselves, and come, all ye heathen, and gather yourselves together round about: thither
cause thy mighty ones to come down, O Lord. Let the
heathen be wakened, and come up to the valley of Jehoshaphat: for there will I set to judge all the heathen round
about. Put ye in the sickle, for the harvest is ripe: come,
get you down; for the press is full, the vats overflow; for
their wickedness is great. Multitudes, multitudes in the
valley of decision; for *the day of the Lord* is near in the
valley of decision. The sun and the moon shall be darkened,
and the stars shall withdraw their shining. The Lord also
shall roar out of Zion, and utter his voice from Jerusalem;
and the heavens and the earth shall shake; but the Lord will
be the hope of his people, and the strength of the children
of Israel. So shall ye know that I am the Lord your God
dwelling in Zion, my holy mountain: then shall Jerusalem be
holy, and there shall no stranger pass through her any more.
Egypt shall be a desolation, and Edom shall be a desolate
wilderness, for the violence against the children of Judah,
because they have shed innocent blood in their land. But
Judah shall dwell forever, and Jerusalem from generation to
generation. For I will cleanse their blood that I have not
cleansed: for the Lord dwelleth in Zion.'' Joel iii, 1, 2,
9–21.

Although the weight of evidence appears to us to
refer these predictions very decisively to the scenes
connected with Israel's final deliverance from her
Gentile oppression, yet, in deference to the opinions
of those expositors, who, on account of the allusions
contained in this chapter of Joel to nations then
dwelling in the neighborhood of the Jews, are dis-
posed to refer them to events then nearer at hand, we
would request our readers, at their pleasure, to pass
them by, as affording, if our view be correct, cumula-
tive evidence only in respect to the circumstances o'
Israel's final deliverance. No doubt, however, is
expressed by the expositors that the prophecies we

shall next quote from the prophet Zechariah clearly
refer to the circumstances of Israel's final deliverance
from Gentile oppression, and to the events which will
follow.

ZECHARIAH :—(Thirty years after Isaiah.)

"The burden of the word of the Lord for Israel, saith
the Lord, which stretcheth forth the heavens, and layeth the
foundations of the earth, and formeth the spirit of man
within him.

"Behold, I will make Jerusalem a cup of trembling unto
all the people round about, when they shall be in the siege
both against Judah, and against Jerusalem.

In that day will I make Jerusalem a burdensome stone for
all people: all that burden themselves with it shall be cut in
pieces, though all the people of the earth be gathered together against it.

In that day, saith the Lord, I will smite every horse with
astonishment, and his rider with madness: and I will open
mine eyes upon the house of Judah, and will smite every
horse of the people [of the besieging nations] with blindness.
And the governors of Judah shall say in their hearts, The
inhabitants of Jerusalem shall be my strength in the Lord of
hosts their God.

"*In that day* will I make the governors of Judah like a
hearth of fire among the wood, and like a torch of fire in a
sheaf; and they shall devour all the people round about, on
the right hand, and on the left; and Jerusalem shall be inhabited again in her own place, even in Jerusalem.

"*In that day* shall the Lord defend the inhabitants of
Jerusalem: and he that is feeble among them at that day
shall be as David; and the house of David shall be a God,
as the angel of the Lord before them, and it shall come to
pass

In that day that I will seek to destroy all the nations
that come against Jerusalem.

*And I will pour upon the house of David, and upon the
inhabitants of Jerusalem, the spirit of grace and of supplications: and they shall look upon me whom they have
pierced, and they shall mourn for him, as one mourneth
for his only son, and shall be in bitterness for him, as one
is in bitterness for his first-born.* Zech. xii, 1–10.

[This passage, last cited, establishes the great
central event in the threefold group, before referred
to, beyond all Scriptural question.]

" *In that day* shall there be a great mourning in Jerusalem, as the mourning of Hadadrimmon in the valley of Megiddon. And the land shall mourn every family apart; the family of the house of David apart, and their wives apart; and the family of the house of Nathan apart, and their wives apart; the family of the house of Levi apart, and their wives apart ; the family of Shimei apart, and their wives apart; all the families that remain, every family apart, and their wives apart." Zech. xii, 11–14.

The description of the Day of the Lord continues; but here we cannot but pause to notice the perfect coincidence of the testimony of our Saviour, and that of the angels who appeared to His sorrowing disciples upon His ascension, and that also of the apostle John in the Revelation, with the above testimony of Zechariah concerning the day of the second coming of Israel's Messiah.

CHRIST:—(seven hundred and fifty years after Isaiah.)

"Immediately after the tribulation of those days, shall the sun be darkened, and the moon shall not give her light, and the stars shall fall from heaven, and the powers of the heavens shall be shaken: *and then shall appear the sign of the Son of Man in heaven: and then shall all the tribes of the land mourn* [not the tribes of the earth in a universal sense, but the tribes of *the land*, of Palestine. of Israel, as see Robinson, Bengel, Tregelles, etc..] *and they shall see the Son of Man coming in the clouds of heaven with power and great glory.*" Matt. xxiv, 29. 30.

"And they [Israel] shall fall by the edge of the sword, and shall be led away captive into all nations ; and Jerusalem shall be trodden down of the Gentiles until the times of the Gentiles shall be fulfilled.

"And there shall be signs in the sun, and in the moon, and in the stars ; and upon the earth distress of nations, with perplexity [not penitential mourning ; that is confined to Israel] ; the sea and the waves roaring; men's hearts failing them for fear, and for looking after those things which are coming on the earth : for the powers of heaven shall be shaken, [Joel iii, 16.] *and then shall they see the Son of Man coming in a cloud with power and great glory.*" Luke xxi, 24–27.

Then is Israel's national redemption at hand.

"And when these things begin to come to pass, then look up, and lift up your heads ; for your redemption draweth nigh." Luke xxi, 28.

So also JOHN, (thirty-six years after Christ.)

"Behold he cometh with clouds ; every eye shall see him, and those who pierced him ; and all the tribes of *the land* shall wail at Him. Even so, Amen." Rev. i, 7.

How can it be Scripturally doubted that the reappearing of the Messiah of Israel, and the consequent mournings of the tribes of Israel, as thus described, are the same described by Zechariah?

So also the angels to the apostles as they beheld the ascension of their blessed Master :—

"Ye men of Galilee, why stand ye gazing up into heaven? this same Jesus which is taken up from you into heaven, shall so come in like manner as ye have seen him go into heaven." Acts i, 11.

Let us now return to the description of Zechariah. We dropped it at the second advent of the Messiah to Israel, and at the universal mourning of the tribes of Israel, when " the Spirit of grace and of supplications shall be poured upon them."

"*In that day* there shall be a fountain opened to the house of David and to the inhabitants of Jerusalem for sin and for uncleanness. And it shall come to pass *in that day* that I will cut off the names of idols out of the land, and they shall no more be remembered." Zech. xiii, 1, 2.

The prophet now reverts to the complete overthrow of the Gentile nations.

" Behold, the day of the Lord cometh, and thy spoil shall be divided in the midst of thee. For I will gather all nations against Jerusalem to battle: and the city shall be taken, and the houses rifled, and the women ravished; and half of the city shall go forth into captivity, and the residue of the people shall be cut off from the city.

"Then shall the Lord go forth, and fight against those nations as he fought in the day of battle.

"And his feet shall stand *in that day* upon the Mount of Olives, which is before Jerusalem. And the Lord shall be king over all the earth, and his name one; and there shall be no more utter destruction; but *Jerusalem shall be safely inhabited.*

"And this shall be the plague wherewith the Lord shall smite all the people that have fought against Jerusalem; Their flesh shall consume away while they stand upon their feet, and their eyes shall consume away in their holes, and their tongue shall consume away in their mouth. And it shall come to pass in that day, that a great tumult from the Lord shall be among them; and they shall lay hold every one on the hand of his neighbor, and his hand shal rise up against the hand of his neighbor." Zech. xiv, 1-3, 9-13.

Thus will close the present dispensation or order of things. Thus will the Messiah return, and Israel be delivered, and her Gentile oppressors be overthrown. Thus will the sentence of judicial blindness expire, and the times of the Gentiles be fulfilled. They will never again obtain ascendency over Israel in the earth, nor national equality with her. They will never seek to obtain it, but will rejoice with Israel in the fulfilment of all her ancient covenants, in the fulfilment of all the holy oaths with which the God of Israel hath ratified and bound them, and in the fulfilment of the predicted blessings which will flow to them therefrom.

It is at this point that the dispensation of judicial prophecy ends, and the dispensation of millennial prophecy, with its full and glowing descriptions of earthly blessedness, begins. It is at this point that the judicial predictions of the public and unexplained parables of our Lord terminate, being all fulfilled: which predictions run in a line strictly parallel, at all points, with the sentence of Israel's judicial blindness. Henceforth and forever more, to the end of the dispensations which are revealed, will restored and redeemed Israel be exalted to the foremost place among the nations of the earth, and dwell safely on the high places of Jacob, among her vines and fig-trees, her olives and her palms: "and all the nations

7*

shall call you blessed, for ye shall be a delightsome land, saith the Lord of hosts" (Mal. iii, 12;) "and their seed shall be known among the Gentiles, and their offspring among the people: all that see them shall acknowledge them, that they are the seed which the Lord hath blessed." Isa. lxi, 9.

Meanwhile, let us, the nations of the Gentiles, lift not up our horn on high; nor speak with a stiff neck, "for promotion cometh neither from the east, nor from the west, nor from the south. *But God is the Judge:* he putteth down one, and setteth up another." Ps. lxxv, 6, 7.

CONCLUSION.

The general conclusion which we would seek to impress upon the minds of our readers, may be briefly stated as follows:—

At the advent, and during the ministry of our Saviour on the earth, the nation of Israel was "concluded in unbelief;" was in a state of judicial blindness, which rendered it impossible for the nation to understand the mysteries of Christ's spiritual kingdom on the earth, under the present Gospel dispensation, as revealed in His public and unexplained parables.

On account of their judicial blindness, they neither would, nor could, nor was it intended that, as a nation, they should, obtain a saving knowledge of these mysteries, until the sentence of their judicial blindness should expire; which sentence, by the very terms in which it was expressed, is to expire only with the expiration of the present Gospel dispensation; or, in other words, when only, and not before, "the fulness of the Gentiles shall come in," or, which is a strictly synonymous expression, when "the times of the Gentiles shall be fulfilled."

Wherefore, it follows, that, until the close of the

present dispensation of God's judicial wrath upon Israel, none of the covenants of blessing which God sware unto the fathers of Israel, can, in any proper, or logical, or Scriptural, or possible sense, in the very nature of things, be said to be fulfilled : without the fulfilment of which covenants of blessing, a millennium, or thousand years, of unmingled and measureless blessing to Israel, and through Israel, to all mankind, is a simply absurd and impossible supposition, whether as viewed in the light of Scripture, or in the light of reason, or in any light whatsoever.

This judicial blindness, which we have endeavored in some measure to explain, is the reason assigned by our Saviour to His disciples why He spake to the nation in parables, explaining them not; which parables are veiled prophecies of the whole course, progress and development of the present judicial dispensation of Israel, in the relation of the Messiah's spiritual kingdom thereto, as affecting Jews and Gentiles both—from the baptism of Christ in the waters of the Jordan, down to that final catastrophe, when He will appear again to overthrow for ever Gentile ascendency and oppression in the earth.

As the judicial blindness of the nation was the reason why they could not understand the veiled meaning of these prophetic parables at the time of our Saviour's ministry, so also, and no less, is it the reason why they have not been able to understand them since, are not able to understand them now, and will not be able to understand them, so long as the appointed term of the sentence of judicial blindness still awaits its expiration.

And as we have found that the *reason* for the use of unexplained parables to the nation is thus prophetic in its character and application; so, as might naturally and Scripturally have been expected, have we also found that these parables were themselves prophetic.

And so will they also appear to Israel, when, at the expiration of her sentence of judicial blindness, "the Spirit of grace and of supplications," so long resisted and blasphemed, and grieved away and quenched, shall be poured upon the house of David, and upon the inhabitants of Jerusalem. Then the veil will be lifted from their eyes. Then the veil will be lifted from these parables; which, each with its train of fulfilled prophecies, will then shine forth to the unclouded vision of redeemed Israel and a redeemed world, as everlasting monuments of the covenanted justice which afflicted, and the covenanted mercy which spared that people, who, whatever their sins and transgressions, are the only covenanted hope of a fallen world.

www.ingramcontent.com/pod-product-compliance
Lightning Source LLC
Chambersburg PA
CBHW021420090426
42742CB00009B/1195